Breathing NEW LIFE *into* LENT

Volume 3

A Collection of Creative Worship Resources

John R. Pritchard Jr.
Anne McKinstry
Janet E. Powers

Judson Press
Valley Forge

Breathing New Life into Lent, Volume 3
A Collection of Creative Worship Resources
© 2000 by Judson Press, Valley Forge, PA 19482-0851
All rights reserved.

Bible quotations in this volume are from the New Revised Standard Version of the Bible, copyright 1989 © by the Division of Christian Education of the National Council of the Churches of Christ in the U.S.A., and are used by permission. All rights reserved.

Library of Congress Cataloging-in-Publication Data

(Updated for Volume 3)
Breathing new life into Lent : a collection of creative worship resources
    Volume 3 authors are John R. Pritchard Jr., Anne McKinstry, and Janet E. Powers
    Volume 2 authors are John R. Pritchard Jr., Anne McKinstry, and Janet E. Powers
    Volume 1 authors are Robert E. Stowe, Donna E. Schaper, Anne McKinstry, and Janet E. Powers
        p. cm.
    1. Lent–Prayer-books and devotions–English. 2. Lenten sermons. 3. Easter service. 4. Easter–Sermons.
    5. Sermons, American. 6. Liturgies. I. Pritchard, John R. Jr.

BV85.B665 2000   98-43639
264–dc21
ISBN 0-8170-1319-9 (pbk. : volume 1)
ISBN 0-8170-1340-7 (pbk. : volume 2)
ISBN 0-8170-1373-3 (pbk. : volume 3)

Printed in the U.S.A.

06   05   04   03   02 01 00
10   9   8   7   6   5   4   3   2   1

Contents

Section III: **NEW SONGS FOR LENT**

Preface

Luke's Gospel gives us a tale of Easter "on the way." The way is specifically a road, the one to Emmaus, and after the events of Easter morning, two disciples are traveling that road away from Jerusalem. These disciples are disappointed in the way life has turned out. The world has proven to be more brutal than they bargained for, chaos more powerful. Their hope has turned out to be more fragile, more easily snuffed out, than they anticipated. So now they walk with the sorrow of all they have lost, the emptiness of all that has been taken from them.

They also journey with confusion. Jesus' tomb was found empty, and the women reported angels who declared him risen, but these disciples do not know what to make of that. So they travel away from it all, away from all that has stung them, that has stolen their hopes and broken their hearts and overwhelmed their minds.

On the way, a stranger joins them, the risen Christ whom they do not recognize. They discuss what has happened; they talk of the Scriptures together; and when they arrive, the disciples implore the stranger to stay with them. At table, he breaks the bread, which is what opens their eyes to recognize him, and they race back to Jerusalem, their hearts burning. They race back to the scene of all they have been fleeing, race back to the life they have been trying to put behind them, their eyes now opened to the One whose life and power they know will meet them there.

That road is an apt image for Lent. Not only is Lent something of a journey itself, a journey toward new life, but that new life happens precisely when our eyes are opened to recognize the presence of Christ with us, the risen One at work in our lives and our world. We bring on that journey our disappointment, our brokenness, all that we sense has gone wrong with us and our world. We also bring our discouragement, the distance between the hopes we had for ourselves, the hopes we sense God has for us, and our reality, the gap between what could be—the *shalom*, the wholeness—and what is.

We also journey with the news that Christ is risen. We know from the beginning where we are headed, how the story will end. It is not new information that we seek on the journey, but new life, life made new by a deeper, richer experience of the risen Christ among us. We journey with the hope that our eyes will be opened, that our hearts will burn within us, that we will meet anew the One at work in our days, calling us to take up that work too in lives of hope and love and praise.

The Lenten journey at its best explores what it is that keeps our eyes closed, what keeps us from recognizing the One who travels with us, what blinds us to the presence of the One who works life and new life. And it prepares us to see anew, to enter our days with new hope, new conviction, new energy, as we join there the risen Christ.

Like the previous volumes, *Breathing New Life into Lent, Volume 3,* offers resources that churches may use as they worship during that journey. Guided by the goal of eye-opened, heart-burning new life, they give voice to our brokenness, to the ways God meets us, and to the life to which God calls us. They are offered with the hope that they may contribute in some small way to breathing new life into the Lenten worship of churches.

Also like the previous volumes, *Breathing New Life into Lent, Volume 3,* contains resources for nine Lenten worship services, from Ash Wednesday through Easter Sunday, all based on the Scripture readings from the Revised Common Lectionary, Year C. Included are three kinds of resources:

Section I: some standard elements of worship (prayers, both congregational and pastoral; responsive calls to worship; children's sermons and sermon ideas)
Section II: prayer dialogues based on antiphonal Scripture readings and metered to be sung or spoken
Section III: original Lenten songs for use in congregational praise and worship or as special music during the worship service

All of these resources are offered with the hope that churches will benefit by using them in whatever way is appropriate in each church's life. Whether an entire worship series is based on these resources or an occasional prayer, song, or sermon idea is borrowed, what matters is that these resources feed the life and worship of churches.

In a sense, the life of the church, the life of faith, is always lived on the road to Emmaus, always lived between the hint of new life and its full, blessed reality. Our eyes are always in need of wider opening, our hearts of deeper encounter, our lives of more daring, loving, living faith. The authors and the staff at Judson Press offer this volume with the hope that it will spark worship that will open our eyes, fire up our hearts, and point us to the risen Christ. As you journey through Lent, we hope that *Breathing New Life into Lent, Volume 3,* will feed your spirit and contribute to worship that calls you from the ways of a death-filled world to the ways of new life in Christ. May it have a hand in inspiring worship that stirs faith large enough, hope wild enough, life bold enough to match the God who trumps death's power and raises life anew.

Section I

WORSHIP SERVICES

by John R. Pritchard Jr.

Dedication

To David and Ian, my sons,
who wear me out but fill me full,
who challenge me daily by their innocence,
their wonder, and their love,

and to Bill Shafer,
whose friendship and whose honest,
struggling faith but deep drink of grace
have long touched my spirit.

Introduction

In this section, Rev. John R. Pritchard Jr. provides the essential elements of nine worship services, beginning with Ash Wednesday and concluding with Easter Sunday. Each service includes opening sentences that serve as a call to worship; an opening prayer that provides a centering theme for the service; a closing prayer, which may be used as an offertory; a prayer of the day to be read by the pastor or in unison by the congregation as a prayer of thanksgiving, intercession, and petition; a children's sermon; and suggestions for a sermon theme based on one of the day's lectionary readings.

Note that many of the prayers are responsive readings in which the leader's voice is in regular typeface and the people's response is in **bold** typeface. Where the leader and people are to respond in unison, the text is prefaced with "ALL" and appears in ***bold and italic*** typeface.

Ash Wednesday

Joel 2:1–2,12–17   *Matthew 6:1–6,16–21*
2 Corinthians 5:20b–6:10   *Psalm 51:1–17*

INTRODUCTION TO THE SERVICE

The ashes of Ash Wednesday are what are left after palms are burned, the same palms that were waved in glad greeting as Christ was welcomed on Palm Sunday. The ashes are a very tangible symbol of joy turned to sorrow, a reminder that the joy of love turns to loss, the joy of life ends in death, the joy of walking in ways that are right falters in our failure to be what we are most called to be. The ashes have traditionally focused on the former, imposed with the words, "Remember you are dust and to dust you return," while the suggested scriptural texts have focused on the latter, calling us to repentance and integrity. Both themes, or either, are appropriate to the day.

These resources are built around the first of those themes, the reminder of our mortality. In facing our brevity, we learn how precious is our time, an insight from which can arise the desire and decision to live it well. Whether used to symbolize mortality or repentance, ashes belong in the service. They may be imposed on the forehead, as is traditional, on the back of the hand, which some find more comfortable, or they may simply be present, a visual reminder of our emptiness without the grace that gives life and reclaims life when the way has been lost.

CALL TO WORSHIP

Leader: We join to praise God.

People: **Breath of Life, to you we cry, "Alleluia!"**

Leader: We gather in the truth that one day we will die.

People: **We stand before the mystery that dwarfs us.**

Leader: It is a fearsome truth,

People: **one we do not manage or control.**

Leader: It is an unbending truth,

People: **one we can neither escape nor avoid.**

Leader: But it is our truth,

People: **one written in us by God.**

Leader: So we come to befriend it,

People: **to treasure the days we have.**

Leader: So we come to face it squarely,

People: **to let go of our fear and grow strong in hope.**

Leader: So we come to find in it a gift,

People: from the God who holds us in life, in death, and beyond.

Leader: To you, O God, we truly cry,

People: "Alleluia! Alleluia!"

CENTERING PRAYER

Gather us, O God, in the grace that gives life.

Strip away our pretensions

    that we are more than we are.

Banish our fears

    that we are less than we are.

        Make your home

        in the heart of who we are,

    that our lives, brief and fragile as they may be,

    will be signs of hope

    and will sing your praise,

    in Christ. Amen.

BLESSING OF THE ASHES

Leader: God is with you.

People: And also with you.

Leader: Let us pray:

    Your wonder is written deep in us, O God.

    We are, by your grace; we are!

People: Blessed are you, O God, Creator of the universe.

Leader: Your breath fills us, O God,

    and then returns to you.

People: Blessed are you, O God, Creator of the universe.

Leader: Grant that these ashes may remind us

    of the dust from which we come

    and to which we return

    and of the great and glorious gift in between.

People: Blessed are you, O God, Creator of the universe.

Leader: Grant that these ashes may remind us

    that we are your people

    and call us again to live in you.

People: Blessed are you, O God, Creator of the universe! Amen.

CLOSING PRAYER

You who give this day,
> and every day,
>> we give thanks for such a gift
>> and we pray for eyes to see its wonder,
>> hearts to cherish its grace,
>> lives shaped by its preciousness,
>> that we may live fully, deeply, lovingly
>> each day we have,
>> in Christ. Amen.

PRAYER OF THE DAY

Spirit wondrous,
> Spirit creative,
>> you are the author of budding spring and of barren winter;
>> you are the mover of rising tides and of ebbing ones;
>> you are the womb of life's beginning
>> and the shroud at life's end.

O God of life's rhythms,
> we come to praise you
>> and to remember again the marvel that we are at all,
>>> by your mercy.

Open our eyes to that gift.
Open our hearts to bathe in its wonder.
Open our mouths to sing your praise.

O God of life's awesome brevity,
> we come to praise you
>> and to savor again the gift of time.

Help us to drink deeply the moments we have,
> to love freely,
> to live fully,
> to walk with you.

O God of life's final breath,
> we come to praise you
>> and to learn with all we are to trust you.

Lean us into your great mystery
> that we might know the love that will not let us go.

O God of all life,
> we come to praise you
>> and to pray your mighty presence wherever life is threatened—
>> by violence, by neglect, by illness or want,

by the slow wasting away of body or spirit.
Breathe anew your healing Spirit
  that our world—and we who fill it—
   might rise again to taste life in its fullness.
O God of life's fierce and glorious mystery,
  we come to praise you:
   Alleluia! Amen.

CHILDREN'S SERMON

Have with you crayons, papers, and ashes. Distribute a crayon and piece of paper to each child. With a crayon, write your initials on a piece of paper. Begin by showing the children your initials, and explain: These are my initials. If I needed to mark something to show that it belonged to me, this is the mark I would use. If you had to mark something to show that it was yours, what kind of mark would you use? Draw it for me.

Give children a short time to draw their marks on their paper. Have them show them, and then ask: What kind of mark would you use to show that something belonged to Jesus?

Again, give the children a short time to draw their marks and to show them. At the same time, draw a cross, and after they have shown their marks, show the cross as the sign the church has often used to show that something belongs to Jesus.

Then show the ashes, and with your finger, stir the ashes and make the mark of the cross on the paper or the back of your hand. Explain: This day is called Ash Wednesday because many churches use ashes to put the sign of the cross on people. That helps them remember that they belong to Jesus, and it helps other people see it too. Unfortunately, the mark comes off as soon as you wash, but the real mark of Jesus is in your heart, and every-day you can remember that you belong to Jesus, and everyday you can show that you belong to him by following his ways.

In congregations that would be comfortable with it, end by placing ashes on the children's forehead or the back of a hand, with words such as, This is the Good News, that you belong to Jesus today and always. In congregations that would not be comfortable with that, simply end with those words, leaving out the ashes.

SERMON MATERIAL

Main Point: Acknowledging our mortality is the beginning of wisdom, the wisdom of accepting our lives as gifts and of living them wisely.

While in graduate school, I taught for several years in the religion department of a large urban university. The course I taught most often was titled simply "Death and Dying." During the years I taught that course, it was interesting to watch people's reactions when they found out what I taught. Some would make a face that showed obvious dis-taste and say, "Oh, how morbid!" Others would say, "Oh, how fascinating!" and then quickly change the subject. Others would simply change the topic as if I said nothing, while some even walked away as if the course content were catching. Few people would ever talk about it at all with me.

All of that is understandable enough. Most of us have our own private fears of dying or of losing those close to us, and we don't like to be reminded of those fears. Nor do we like to think and talk about what is so patently unpleasant.

On the other hand, Christians have long said that it is important to remember that we will die, that there is something significant in recalling that our journey here is a brief one. One thing that has freed them to remember that is the hope that our journey will be renewed with the resurrected Christ, but another reason for such honesty about our death is that Christians have long claimed that such honesty leads to wisdom about ourselves, to a wisdom that fits us for living.

The New Testament is full of passages that name the brevity of time and call for a new wisdom, a renewed living, a renewed commitment in that light. "Behold, now is the acceptable time; behold, now is the day of salvation," writes Paul, pointing to the shortness of time and the incredible importance of today. "What is your life? For you are a mist that appears for a little time and then vanishes," writes James, calling for a new humility in the face of passing time. "Which of you by being anxious can add one cubit to the span of your life?" asks Jesus, reminding his hearers that our journey is brief. That recognition is not the cause of despair, however, but the occasion for new living—"Seek first God's kingdom and God's righteousness. . . ."

What lies at the heart of such passages is the invitation to the wisdom that comes from an honest acknowledgment of our mortality, a wisdom that looks at our lives in new perspective and learns to cherish what should be cherished, to give importance to what is important, and to treat lightly what should be treated lightly. In essence, at the heart of such passages is the reminder that there is wisdom in knowing our time is short, a wisdom that restrains us from wasting time or being consumed by empty things, a wisdom that leads us to give our love to what is worth loving and to give our time to what is worth our time. "Seek first God's kingdom and God's righteousness. . . ."

Christians have always thought that our priorities change and we have our lives in new perspective when we acknowledge the shortness of our journey. And therefore Christians have always had times to remind themselves of death, of the brevity of life, times to seek the wisdom that leads to new living. One of those times is Lent, our journey to the death of Jesus. It is a journey that begins today in acknowledging our own death. The tradition of the church is to be marked with ashes on this day, ashes that are imposed with the words, "Remember that you are dust, and to dust you return."

That may at first strike you as morbid, but it is rather an invitation to wisdom, an invitation to live fully, wisely, richly, and lovingly the brief and precious gift of life God gives us.

As we begin our Lenten journey together, I pray that we will again have a taste of that wisdom and that we will discover the new life that comes from it.

First Sunday in Lent

Deuteronomy 26:1–11   *Luke 4:1–13*
Romans 10:8b–13   *Psalm 91:1–2, 9–16*

CALL TO WORSHIP

Leader: In the great grace of God, welcome.

People: God's peace be yours.

Leader: Today we begin our Lenten journey,
a journey that will take us to the cross
and to the empty tomb beyond.

**People: We will wade into the mystery of dying
and of rising with new life.**

Leader: We begin by following Jesus into the wilderness,
a barren and lonely place.

People: We acknowledge so much that is barren in our lives.

Leader: We stand beside Jesus during his long fast,
as he grows weak and hungry.

**People: We admit our own weakness,
the need inside us.**

Leader: We remain with Jesus as he is tempted,
as he wrestles with desire.

**People: We know there is so little wrestling in us
because we all too easily yield to desire,
hoping to satisfy our every want.**

Leader: We marvel at the peace of this Jesus,
a calm center rooted in God.

**People: We yearn for such peace in our lives,
and so we pray:
Plant our hearts in you, O God.
Grow us into steady faith,
in Christ. Amen.**

CENTERING PRAYER

You who part the sea,
    impart the manna,
    shatter exile's grasp;
You who embrace the outcast,
    heal the sick,
    open the tomb:
Yours is the work of freeing your people
    from all that diminishes life,
    and we praise you.
    Today we ask your blessing on us.
As we worship together,
    pray together,
    read your Scriptures together,
    and consider your ways,
    reach into our midst.
Touch and stir us.
Loosen the grip of all that holds us prisoner
    to lives that are less than you want for us.
Help us rise—
    to work, to dream, to laugh, to love—
    in the great power of your Spirit,
    through Christ. Amen.

CLOSING PRAYER

O God,
    you feed us in our wilderness
    and wrap us in your love.
Now send us in your Spirit
    to hope in you,
    to love like you,
    to give praise to you.
Alleluia! Amen.

PRAYER OF THE DAY

We come to this place, O God, as to a wilderness—
 a time apart, a place apart, a chance to be alone with you.
As we gather, as we wait in your presence,
  ready us, we pray, for the new life you bring,
  to us and to your world.
Where we have lost our vision, where our dreams have grown small,
  where our hopes have shrunk to the size of promises made in advertisements,
  breathe on us again,
  that we may grow large in your life
  and have hopes for our world large enough to match your creative power.
Where we have grown more fearful than faithful,
  more committed to the way things are than the way they should be,
  more intent on preserving our lives than daring life in abundance,
  stoke in us anew your great passion for life made whole,
  that we might rise as your people and join in your work.
Where we have denied the voice we have, the strength you give,
  the gifts with which you endow us for the sake of your world,
  where we dismiss ourselves as incapable of making a difference
  and wait always for someone else to act,
  stir us with your Spirit
  to claim the power you pour into each of us.
Ready us to be the people you call us to be,
  to do the work you call us to do,
  to live life as abundantly as you yearn for us to live it.
Pour out your Spirit wherever life is broken,
  where dreams have become nightmares or love grown violent,
  where hearts or hopes or stomachs are empty.
Pour out your Spirit wherever life groans to be made new
  or has long since fallen mute.
Pour out your Spirit and begin your work of healing.
As we come to this place as to a wilderness,
  as we begin our Lenten journey to the new life you bring,
  ready us, ready our world, to rise in your ways
  and laugh with your praise,
  in Christ. Amen.

CHILDREN'S SERMON

How many of you have ever gone away on vacation? How many of you have ever started back to school after a summer of being at home? How many of you have ever celebrated a big holiday like Christmas? *By now everyone should have raised his or her hand to indicate yes.*

What kind of things do you do to get ready, to get prepared for any of those? *Let the children answer, but prompt them if you need to, aiming toward ideas like packing, buying supplies, putting up decorations, wrapping gifts.*

What do you think you might do to get ready to be a disciple, to follow Jesus? *Let the children answer. If they have no answers, you might prompt them with suggestions such as, "Learn about Jesus. Read the Bible. Pray." Don't get bogged down here, though.*

Jesus spent some time preparing before he began his work. He went into the wilderness where he could be alone to decide what was important for him to do and just how he would carry on his ministry.

The season of Lent is about deciding what is important. But that's also what every day is about. Every morning and at other times throughout the day we have to decide "Will I follow Jesus today? Will I do what Jesus would want me to do? Will I love others like Jesus does? Will I try to do what is right? Will I try to be close to God? Will I listen for what God says to me?"

Just like Jesus had to get ready, so do we. Every day we prepare for what will happen that day by deciding whether we will spend the day with Jesus.

Today, will you?

SERMON MATERIAL (Luke 4:1–13)

Main Point: Lent is a time for refocusing, for examining our lives and deciding what is important. The questions Jesus wrestled with in the wilderness are questions that can apply to us and prod our spiritual growth.

As Lent began one year, a friend and I were talking, and knowing I am a pastor, he turned the conversation to Lent. "I'm giving up shark meat for Lent," he told me.

I thought he was pulling my leg, so I chuckled and said, "I know. You don't like it, so it's no problem to give up."

"No, I love it," he protested, and I thought for a moment we might really be talking about an attempt at disciplined fasting and self-reflection. But then he continued, "I love it, but I rarely get to eat it. I figured that would make it easy to skip for a few weeks."

That exchange pretty much sums up what little meaning is left in Lent in many places. It is about giving up something, who knows why, just give it up—and the easier the better! It has been trivialized, as has much that has to do with our spirits.

But the point of Lent has never been to give up something. That has been one of the disciplines, one of the spiritual exercises used, but the point is not the giving up; the point is what giving up enables us to do—to refocus, to tune in to our spirits, to listen to our depths and hear what they're saying about us and about God. The word Lent originally meant "spring," and Lent was a time of reflection to prepare for the new life spring brings, a time to burrow deep into the soil of our lives and wait there like seeds for the rebirth that comes with spring.

You get a sense of that inwardness and refocusing in the fact that each year Lent begins with the gospel account of Jesus in the wilderness. The wilderness is a highly symbolic place in Scripture, and its meanings are many. It is a place of tragedy, where wildness overtakes us. It is a place of testing, in the way Israel's trust in God was tested as they had to wait for food and water and guidance there. It is a place of purification, as Israel was purified of the habits of slavery and the fear of new life and was prepared for a new land by wandering in the wilderness for forty years. It is a place of creativity, a place where the settled ways of civilization hold no sway and new ways can be envisioned, new dreams dreamed. For Luke, it is a place of decision, which is why Jesus goes there immediately after his baptism but before he begins his ministry. There he sorts through the options he has for the shape his ministry will take—will he be a social worker who feeds the hungry, a politician who seeks power to wield for the good, a spectacle-maker and wonder-worker who can win an audience? These are all very real directions he can take, and what he is doing in the wilderness is wrestling with his direction, the most authentic, appropriate, healing direction he can take. He is deciding the path he will walk, the shape of his holy work. Wilderness is the place where he sharpens his focus so that his ministry can begin when he returns to civilization. Wilderness is where he germinates and then blossoms into new life in the mission he takes up.

All of this is a reminder of what Lent can be for us—a time to germinate; a time to question ourselves; a time to be questioned; a time to listen into our lives and ask how we are faring, where we are going, where we would like to go, what we need; a time to touch base with the deeper parts of ourselves and inquire about their health and well-being and listen to what they might say about our living. Whether or not Lent becomes that for us, we all need times to listen deeply to ourselves, times to examine our direction, times to turn our eyes inward to prepare for new life.

Given that we all need such times, it would be wise to let Lent become such a time for us, and one way to start is to spend a few minutes with the questions Jesus wrestled with in the wilderness, questions that we all face at some time and answer in some way. Though for Jesus they were questions primarily about his ministry, they're also questions about values, about what is important, about how we live and what we live for.

The first question has to do with the need for bread and whether Jesus will reduce his ministry to providing bread for those who have none. For many in the church, bread isn't an issue—we have enough to eat, enough, at least, to survive. But the question does address us in terms of how much we reduce our lives to things—to trips to the mall and the whole consumer package, to our dream house, to the latest gadgets for ourselves or our kids, to our new clothes or new hairdo or new cars, to our savings or investments, to what we have or own or buy. Do we feed our hunger for meaning with the junk food of trinkets?

You're not alone if you do reduce your life to things. Our culture bombards us with its sacred messages—advertisements—telling us that is the right thing to do, and to our detriment we listen. How many of us can't stop wanting or buying or using or eating, or you name it? How many of us just keep reaching for things to fill the emptiness inside us, an emptiness that isn't an enemy but a friend, an invitation, calling us into the presence of God, who alone can fill that void?

Whether we can't stop, we're addicted, or we just have too much stuff in our lives, the same questions are raised, questions like those Jesus faced. Have we reduced ourselves to things, sacrificed the life of our spirit to them? Do we attend to our spiritual lives? Do we spend as much time and energy on our search for meaning and grace and beauty and wonder and compassion as we do going to the mall or watching television? Are we as serious about the life of our spirits as we are about buying a new car? Do we take time to listen to our depths, to feed and stretch our spirits, to grow in God, or are we dying, as Dorothee Soelle called it, by bread alone, starving in all our stuff?

The second question Jesus wrestled with was the invitation to take all the glory and power of the kingdoms so he could use them for good, which is an invitation we certainly rarely receive. But we face the same question in our desire to be somebody or in our fear of being nobody, in our sense that we are nothing if we don't stand out or don't belong to the right group or church or circle of friends, in our need to prove ourselves or to look good in the eyes of others. The glory we seek may be meager, but it's glory nonetheless.

Jesus cuts through it all by saying we should worship God alone, meaning that our value, our belonging, is in trusting in the love and esteem with which God holds us. How do we value ourselves? Do we measure ourselves against some standard of accomplishment, of right belief, of social fitness, of moral decency? Do we spend our lives trying to prove ourselves to others? Do we live with the haunting sense that we can't even do that, that we can never really matter to anyone, that we can't be good enough or smart enough or attractive enough or "normal" enough? Do we value ourselves at all, or do we live with the sense that we don't matter, that our lives are unimportant, that our point of view or decisions or actions aren't worth a hoot? Do we dismiss ourselves, or are we able to trust the God who makes us in God's image and calls us sons and daughters?

Jesus says to worship God alone, which means to trust the worth that God gives us regardless of who we are or what we've done or what we've failed to do, to know we're somebody because we are somebody to God. So can we affirm our dignity, our glory, or must we sell our souls, give up ourselves, to find value in others' eyes?

The final question Jesus wrestled with was his desire to give up responsibility for his ministry, to take a short-cut, to dazzle the crowds and become an instant hit by throwing himself off the temple and letting angels come to rescue him. Now, without a doubt, few of us are faced with that question so dramatically, but in some form it does address us all. Does our faith encourage us to take responsibility for ourselves, our lives, our world, or does it encourage us to give up responsibility, to dismiss ourselves, to remain passive? Is God the source of our strength or an excuse for irresponsibility? Do we expect too much of God and too little of ourselves?

We learn in Sunday school that God is in charge, that God has a hand in everything and will take care of us and never let us face more than we can handle, which are comforting thoughts very appropriate for a child. But as we grow up, as our abilities mature, a faith that stays at that level remains childish and is no longer appropriate. It stunts the growth of our spirits, dulls the edge of God's call to a mature life and faith, not to mention that it doesn't fit our experience—that God doesn't save us from our foolishness or protect us from the consequences of our decisions, that God isn't the quick fix for every problem or the safety net that cushions us from falling or the cosmic daddy who makes everything better.

Early in my ministry, during the energy crisis of the 1970s when the first widespread awareness arose of the collision course between the limited resources of our planet and our gluttonous lifestyles, an adult Sunday school class I was part of talked about ways of living more responsibly and using less energy. Turning down the heat was suggested, as was driving less and using public transportation more. Finally, one young woman spoke up, telling us our whole conversation was a waste of time. "If we use up this planet," she said, "God will give us another one."

That's the issue Jesus wrestled with in the wilderness—expecting too much of God, expecting the miracle—no, magical—answer, using faith to dismiss us from mature living, using faith as an excuse for not taking responsibility for the way we live, the ways we treat ourselves and others, the ways we care and give and offer ourselves. That's the issue Jesus faced and that faces us all. Does our faith encourage our maturity or detract from it? Does our faith empower us or belittle us? Does our faith grow us into the partners God calls us, or does it trap us in spiritual childhood?

Those are the questions with which Jesus wrestled in the wilderness and with which we all wrestle on our spiritual journeys, especially during Lent, a time for redirecting our lives. I hope Lent can become a time like that for each of us this year. In fact, it would be good to end with just a few moments of silence, time to be still with God and to listen to the thoughts that come to you, thoughts about your life and the questions we've faced here, thoughts about ways you might attend more to your spiritual life, ways you might embrace the worth God gives you, ways you might rise to your partnership with God. Listen for them, and in the silence of these moments make a commitment—not for a lifetime, but simply for the six weeks of Lent, from now until Easter. Let that commitment be your Lenten discipline, the ground from which God can grow new life.

Second Sunday in Lent

Genesis 15:1–12, 17–18   Luke 13:31–35
Philippians 3:17–4:1   Psalm 27

CALL TO WORSHIP

Leader: In the great grace of God, welcome.

People: God's peace be yours.

Leader: Today we continue our Lenten journey,
a journey that will take us to the cross
and to the empty tomb beyond.

**People: We will wade into the mystery of dying
and of rising with new life.**

Leader: Today we will hear of covenant,
of citizenship, of commitment larger than fear.

**People: We will ask where our hearts stand,
where our loyalties lie.**

Leader: We will consider the work God is doing
and examine ourselves in its light.

**People: Against the yardstick of God's ways,
we will measure our own.**

Leader: We will ask if there is any flavor of the new life God brings

People: (Can anyone see in us something of Christ?)

Leader: or the love God works

People: (Does our living tell the tale of God's unyielding love for all?)

Leader: And we will pray that God
touch and claim us anew.

**People: Plant our hearts in you, O God.
Grow us into Christ,
into a life and love like yours. Amen.**

CENTERING PRAYER

Holy One,

> we gather as those pulled in so many directions
> that our lives are stretched exceedingly thin
>> and ready to break.

So many voices clamor for us to buy their products,

> so many voices tell us how to do everything
> and tell us we are wrong if we don't do it their way,
> so many voices cry for help
> and demand our time, our money, our energy,
> that we begin to lose our way among them
> and lose ourselves among them.

So we gather here,

> not knowing where to turn,
> afraid that yours will be simply one more voice making demands on us,
> but hoping that in you we may rest and be renewed.

O you who gather the outcasts home,

> gather us to your breast.

Restore us in your strong embrace.

Center our hearts in you

> that we may face all that pulls us this way and that
> with the calm assurance of your grace
> and the deep strength of your Spirit.

We ask this in Christ's name. Amen.

CLOSING PRAYER

Gracious God,

> you adopt us as citizens of your realm,
> where hope and love abound.

By your Spirit, shape our lives

> until they conform to the home of our citizenship,
> in Christ. Amen.

PRAYER OF THE DAY

You who would gather us under your wings and mother us,
>   we come to you.

From a world long on promises but short on the ability to deliver,
>   we come.

From a world bloated with things but small of heart,
>   we come.

From a world fat with wealth but thin of spirit,
>   we come.

Nourish us with your life.
>   Where we run and run, yet know no peace,
>   give us rest in your Spirit.

Where we ache over yesterday or fret over tomorrow,
>   so that we are paralyzed today,
>   set us free in your Spirit.

Where we yearn to matter but cannot see beyond our own small concerns,
>   grow us in your Spirit
>   until our hearts are large enough to beat for your world and all your people.

In a world that tries so many new things
>   but has long forgotten how to dare anything really important,
>   let loose your love that we might feed the hungry and clothe the naked
>   and give place and life to those who have none.

In a world that is constantly developing new products
>   but has long forgotten how to dare anything really important,
>   let loose your Spirit that we might beat swords into plowshares
>   and learn neither war nor terror nor abuse anymore,
>   but unleash our energies to create, to build up, to flourish together.

In a world that is endlessly funding new research
>   but has long forgotten how to dare anything really important,

let loose your life that we might tend your earth and plant and preserve
>   and see deserts blossom and wastelands sprout beauty.

You who would gather us under your wings and mother us,
>   we come to you.

We bring ourselves. We bring our world.

We bring all that needs your life-giving touch.

Nourish us in the wonder of your presence,
>   O God of life. Amen.

CHILDREN'S SERMON

Have with you something that serves as a security blanket for you or someone else. Explain what it is and what it does. I would take the infant sweater that my son has had for years that he holds to comfort him for sleep and picks up whenever he is upset or frightened. Or I would simply tell what happens when I go ice skating—how I love to skate but am so afraid of falling that I hold on to the wall the whole time. After you tell about your security blanket, then ask the children about theirs.

Do you have anything that you like to hold on to? Anything that makes you feel safe? Anything you're afraid to let go of? *Give them time to answer. Be prepared for anything.*

Most of us have something that makes us feel a little safer, a little less afraid. The Bible tells the story of a time when some people came to Jesus and wanted him to hold on to *the wall/the blanket (use images they have raised)* to play it safe. "The king's out to get you," they told him, wanting him to hide away, to get out of sight. But do you know what he told them? "I'm going to continue my work until I'm done," he said.

Jesus found something more important than playing it safe, something bigger than the fear inside him, and that was doing what was right, doing what God wanted him to do. So another way for us to feel a little less afraid is to do what God wants us to do. That doesn't mean things won't go wrong, that they'll always turn out right, but it does mean you'll walk a little closer to God, who is bigger than any fear.

SERMON NOTES (Genesis 15:1–12, 17–18; Luke 13:31–35)

Main Point: God's unconditional love can free us from the anxiety that causes us to play it safe, free us to take risks in our lives, and free us to dare something holy.

Anyone who watched the 1998 Winter Olympics was treated to high drama in the figure skating championships. Two young women, both American, were vying for the gold medal. On the one hand was Michelle Kwan, seasoned some since her first appearance at the Olympics four years earlier but still only seventeen years old. She was technically gifted and had a mature, artistic style; she was so talented and fluid in motion that she was considered a shoo-in for the gold. On the other hand was Tara Lipinski, only fifteen, whose young age showed a bit in her art but could not take away from the fact that she was an incredibly talented technician. Through the events they held their places, Michelle in first, Tara in second, and then came the final event. Michelle was still in the lead, having done so well that everyone said all she had to do was make no mistakes, and that's just what she did—made no mistakes, skated flawlessly, perhaps a bit safely, but perfectly. Then came Tara, following after perfection, and she pulled out all the stops, skated boldly, dared jumps that others don't even do during competition, and did them flawlessly. She won because she took risks.

Commentators said Tara had nothing to lose, which is what freed her to skate with abandon, courage, and sheer joy. Michelle, on the other hand, had everything to lose. You could tell that from her response to winning the silver medal, the medal naming her the second best in the world. The news reported that she said to her family and coach, "I hope you still love me!"

Their competition was drama at its best, but it was more than that. The dance, the tension, the pull between them is the pull that defines our lives so often, and I wonder which of them our lives resemble more. Is your life more like Michelle's or Tara's? Are you the one to play it safe, to be protective, to sacrifice the heights you dream of for the security of knowing you are aiming within your reach, or do you take the risks, go for broke, push the envelope? Do you hold back, cover your bases, yield to anxiety or fear, or do you let loose, push through the fears, and taste the freedom of nothing to lose? Which are you?

That same dance, that same pull, runs through our Scripture readings for this day. The gospel gives the same two models—those calling Jesus to play it safe, to keep his head down, to hang on to what he has, in this case his skin, and Jesus himself, throwing caution to the wind, going for broke, stepping out with abandon as he dares to go his way whatever Herod says or does. It's the same conflict between anxiety and faith and which one will set the agenda, between the fear of losing everything and the freedom of having nothing to lose and which one will determine his way.

Abram experienced the same dance. He had already gone for broke, stepped out in faith, left everything to chase the dream God had given him. But now he was having second thoughts, wondering if he had been a fool and questioning God's reliability. Now doubt was settling in, anxiety was rising, and the desire to play it safe was growing strong. The dance was inside him until God stepped in.

What happened next is bizarre to modern ears. We stumble over the strange, gory imagery—a goat cut in two and hung up, Abram sleeping, and God passing between the hunks of meat as smoke and fire. We trip over the weirdness of it, and ancient people tripped over this story too, but for different reasons. The ritual made no one stumble; it was as commonplace as a handshake or signing on the dotted line is today. It was the way of sealing a covenant. In fact, it is where the phrase "cutting a bargain" or "cutting a deal" comes from. The person making the covenant passed between the two halves of a slain animal with words to the effect, "May the same or worse happen to me if I fail to keep my promise."

No one in Abram's day would have tripped over the gory details of the story. What caught them up short and caused them to shake their heads, what stood out as completely out of place, was how one-sided the covenant was, how generous or crazy this God was. Abram slept; God cut a bargain. Abram did nothing; God gave a promise. Abram owed nothing; God owed everything, no matter what!

Deals are supposed to be fifty-fifty. You do this for me, and I'll do that for you. You'd have to be a fool to ask nothing in return, but that's what God did—God asked nothing in return and expected nothing in return. God gave God's self to Abram for free. God would be Abram's God, would be with Abram and love Abram, for free. Abram had nothing to lose, because God's love would not let go.

It strikes me as ironic that we stumble over the things in this story that the ancients took for granted, the bizarre and gory details, while they stumbled over exactly what we take for granted, this claim of God's love no matter what, a claim we've heard so often that it means little. God loves you, God loves you, God loves you—we've heard it so much we barely even notice it, and yet I wonder if we've ever really heard it. In the part of us that still needs to prove ourselves, have we heard it? In the part of us that stings with shameful memories or limps with a sense of inadequacy, that just knows we don't measure up, have we heard it? In the part of us that trembles with fear or shrinks with anxiety or hides our neediness behind a smiling face, have we heard it? Does it matter? This claim that God loves us, that God says to us, "I won't give you up; I won't leave you; I won't stop loving you—ever"? This claim that we have nothing to lose, nothing we can lose, because God won't let go? Does it matter?

Only you can answer that for yourself, but I suspect it could matter to a friend of mine, a young man in his early thirties, a salesman in a highly competitive field who had been having a bit of a difficult time at work. He came home one night not feeling well and went to bed early, but before long his wife heard strange sounds coming from their room and ran to find out what was wrong. She found her husband writhing on their bed, torn by huge wrenching sobs. As she wrapped him in her arms, he cried out, "Will you love me if I fail?"

Does it matter that God loves us and won't stop? I suspect it could to the students of an Ivy League university that offered a new course listing a few years ago entitled "How to Deal with Failure." The course drew enrollment beyond all expectations; no matter how many sections of the course were added, each one filled up immediately. The response made it clear that the high-achieving, gifted students there hadn't the foggiest idea how to face failure or the anxiety it raised in them.

Does it matter that God loves us no matter what? I suspect it could to a man I once talked with, an alcoholic, a talented man who had a great deal going for him, a great deal on the line, but all of it at risk because of his uncontrolled drinking. We talked about support groups, about AA. He said he went once a month, but it hadn't helped much. He just couldn't talk there, couldn't really say anything. When I asked him why, he sobbed, "I'm too ashamed. No one will love me if they see how weak I am."

Does it matter that God loves us unconditionally? I suspect it could matter to those of us who have been taught all our lives that we'll be okay if we're only good enough or smart enough or make enough money. And it could matter to those of us who have learned that God will love us or bless us if we do this or that, if we do not do this or that, if we believe this or that. I suspect it could make a difference to know that with God there is no "if"; with God there is only a "yes," to us!

Does it matter that God won't let go? I suspect it did matter to Jesus when he was informed that one of the most powerful and most brutal rulers around wanted his skin; he was probably tempted to slink off and stay safe, to give in to his fear. But something else mattered, mattered enough for him to tell the fox to take a hike and for him to go on doing his loving work.

Does it matter? I suspect it did to Martin Luther King and so many with him, who withstood vicious dogs, hateful mobs, fire hoses, white sheets, painful clubs, firebombs, and lynchings. I suspect it does to a group of young Christians so concerned about education and poverty and God's love for all that they are willing to put themselves on the line. Committed families enter the worst neighborhoods in the nation to live and to set up schools where kids from the poorest families can have a place to learn, where kids from even the most dysfunctional families are loved, are taught, and have a safe place. The schools survive by getting donations and because the staff lives on poverty wages. What does it take to move your family into poverty, live with them there at risk, and do it for next to nothing except the chance to love someone else?

I suspect it takes something that matters, a love that won't let you go, a love that holds you no matter what, a love that you can't lose. It takes a love like God's, who cuts a deal with you, a deal to love you no matter what, a deal to love you and that's that! No questions asked, nothing expected in return, just to love you!

Does it matter? To you? Let's pray that it does. Let's pray that at the heart of all of us it does, that we'll taste what it is to be loved, that we'll know how to be free, that we'll know what it is to have nothing to lose because God won't let go!

Third Sunday in Lent

Isaiah 55:1–9 *Luke 13:1–9*
1 Corinthians 10:1–13 *Psalm 63:1–8*

CALL TO WORSHIP

Leader: In the great grace of God, welcome.

People: God's peace be yours.

Leader: We continue on our Lenten journey,
a journey that will take us to the cross
and to the empty tomb beyond.

**People: We will wade into the mystery of dying
and of rising with new life.**

Leader: Today we will dip into the mystery
of a God whose ways are not our ways.

**People: We will face a God
whose love is without boundary or condition.**

Leader: We will swim into the mystery of life's unfairness,
of good and ill undeserved.

**People: We will face our nakedness,
our exposure to harms we cannot control.**

Leader: We will plunge into the mystery of tragedy
and the suffering it works in us.

**People: We will face into senselessness
and hope still to find God.**

Leader: We bring our souls, hungering and thirsting,
unsatisfied by the world's diet.

**People: And so we pray:
Plant our hearts in you, O God.
Grant us faith
to lean into the shadow of your presence,
to trust where we cannot see,
to stand and hope when we've been flattened,
and finally, finally, to praise you:
Alleluia! Amen.**

CENTERING PRAYER

Holy Mystery,
    you hold all creation in your heart,
    you send sun and rain on just and unjust alike,
    you are vast in compassion, gracious in mercy,
and we praise you,
    even while we admit that
    we have learned to see all things through
    the narrow eyes of our desires, our wants.
We value things—people, policies, events—
    by how they affect our wishes,
    and we have lost the art of finding you and your grace
    where we least expect to.
Teach us anew, Gracious Mystery.
Give us hearts convinced of your grace
    and eyes intent to find it.
Grow our hearts until they are large enough to have room
    for what we neither understand nor appreciate.
You hold us in your heart, Loving Mystery.
Teach our hearts to hold on to you,
    in Christ. Amen.

CLOSING PRAYER

You, O God, are
    moving wind, flowing sea, swirling mist,
    shadowed and elusive, ever beyond our grasp,
    and yet, at heart, grace unbounded,
    love without measure.
Grant us faith to lean into the fog
    and rest in you,
    through Christ. Amen.

PRAYER OF THE DAY

We come, O God, as those who thirst,
> from a world that has failed to satisfy us.

Though we run and run, though we work and work,
> though we have and have,
> yet we are still empty.

So we come to you.
Give us drink, we pray.

Though we swim in a sea of information,
> yet we thirst for simple wisdom.

Though we bob in a sea of options,
> yet we thirst to know what really matters.

Though we float in an ocean of people,
> yet we thirst for real human contact,
> for love and understanding.

Though we drown in an ocean of things,
> yet we still thirst for something
> to ease the ache within us.

So we come to you.
Give us drink, we pray.

Where we have misspent our time,
> redirect us.

Where we have mishandled your world,
> release us from the folly of our ways.

Where we have mistreated your children,
> refashion our ways in the way of your love.

Where we have been mistaken about what will
> bring joy and satisfaction,
> reclaim us, that we might rest in you.

You who are the bread that can sustain us,
> the wine that can delight us,
> we come to you as those who thirst.

From the fountain of your presence,
> give us drink,
> that your life may flow through us
> and our lives may know what it is to be full.

Give us drink, O God,
> until we overflow with a love like yours
> and with praise of you. Amen.

CHILDREN'S SERMON

Have you ever had a bad day? Have you ever had a terrible, no-good day? A time when everything seemed to go wrong? When nothing went your way? *Give them time to answer. Encourage their telling of stories of those days. If it fits and their stories aren't too long, tell your own story of a horrible day. I would tell of a recent day when my wife got sick, then got feeling so bad we had to go to the hospital, where she was admitted. Later in the day, on the way to see her, I ran into another car and ruined my own car.*

How did you feel? I know how I felt, like everything had turned against me, like God was gone or was punishing me.

We all feel that way sometimes. In fact, people in Jesus' day felt that way, too. The Bible tells a story of a day when a group came to Jesus asking if God was punishing some people who had experienced really bad things.

Do you know what Jesus did? He ignored them! At least he didn't answer their questions. Instead, he asked them if they were living right. He was so sure that God loves us, that God doesn't give us up or turn against us, that he had no doubts about it. That's why he didn't answer them.

We all have pretty bad days sometimes, and we all have some pretty rotten feelings when we do. But maybe we can learn a lesson from Jesus and remember, even then, that God loves us and won't let us go.

SERMON MATERIAL (Luke 13:1-9)

Main Point: Jesus' response to those who came questioning who was to blame for some tragedies undercuts a bookkeeper view of God, where we control our destinies by good or bad living. He points instead toward the mystery of grace and uses tragedy to question us all.

I doubt there is one of us here who hasn't, at one time or another, asked the question those folks were asking Jesus. Some tragedy, some pain, some senseless accident happens, and we find ourselves driven to sort it out, driven to make some sense of it. "Why?" we ask. "Why?"—which is the question they came asking Jesus.

In one incident a group of Galileans came to the temple in Jerusalem to worship, but they were met there by Pilate's henchmen, who brutally slaughtered them. In another incident, a tower, which was part of the aqueduct in Siloam, fell over, and eighteen people were crushed to death. The survivors were left to sort through the seemingly senseless tragedy and to put the pieces together, left to try to make sense of it all. "Why?" they came asking Jesus.

Many answers have been given to such questions, answers we've probably heard, answers we may have given ourselves. "He never did wear his seat belt," is the comment I heard someone make at the funeral of a young man killed in a terrible car crash, implying that it was somehow his fault, that he did something wrong. A seat belt would have made no difference whatsoever in this case, but the person was trying to give the accident some sense—it was fair; he deserved it.

That's a common answer people give to suffering; they look for some place to lay the blame, some way the victims deserved their fate. It's the answer many have given to the suffering of those with AIDS and one of the reasons it took us so long to respond to the AIDS crisis with funding for medical research and care. It's the answer so many give to the suffering of poverty—it's not our responsibility; it's theirs; they deserve it, somehow. It's the answer brought by those who questioned Jesus in this story, those who wondered if the victims were terrible sinners, if somehow they deserved to die.

That's a common answer, an easy answer, one that makes sense of the tragedy at the same time that it leaves us feeling safe and in control. Such horror won't happen to us, because we're not like them, because we don't do that, because we don't deserve it. That's what makes it such a powerful answer; it helps us feel protected in the midst of the hurricane, as if we have some control over the chaos of our lives.

That's a powerful answer we give, but there are others. One has less to do with others than with ourselves. "God is testing me, testing my faith," we say, or, "God has a lesson for me to learn." I once ministered to a woman who was battling breast cancer. At one point as she wrestled with her illness, she went to a healing service in a church. She wasn't cured, and she came to see me, telling me, with tears and deep pain, that her faith must not be strong enough. It was her fault that she remained sick, she thought, because she failed God's test.

How terrified we must be when we need to blame ourselves or cling to a punishing, vindictive, taskmaster God in order to make sense of our lives. How great must be our pain, how deep our fear!

Still another answer we give for our suffering admits our own smallness. "God has a reason, and we can't question it," we say, despite the fact that precisely what we are having a hard time believing at the moment is that God does have a reason and what we can't seem to stop doing is questioning. Sometimes we say it all the more or all the louder, as if just repeating it will convince us and quiet us down, as if God prefers our quiet to our questions, as if God is afraid of our probing.

Whatever reasons we give, we all know how those who came to Jesus felt. We know the shudder that runs through us after some senseless event—after the evening news carries an image of the aftermath of a bomb or a plane crash or a flood or fire, after a child dies senselessly or you lose a loved one or a sudden illness knocks you flat or an accident rips open your happy world. We know what it is to feel helpless and vulnerable, to want to find some reason behind it all, to want to find some way to feel safe and sure that such a thing can't happen to us. We know what it is to ask, "Why?"

Knowing that, I am struck by the fact that in the story Jesus never answers his inquirers' question. "Why?" they ask, and Jesus replies, "Do you think they were worse sinners than everyone else? No, and unless you repent you will likewise perish." They come asking why, trying to make sense out of what has happened to others, and Jesus turns the question on them: "You, too, will perish. Repent."

One way to understand that is to think that we all deserve such suffering, that God is in the business of running about and punishing sinners, that we'd better get our act together or God will get us. There are plenty of preachers who read the story that way, preachers who are perfectly content to scare folks into the kingdom: repent or else! Or else you'll get yours!

Although many people read the story that way, there's a problem with such a reading. It leaves us with the same illusion that those who came to Jesus had in the first place, the mistaken notion that God is the Great Accountant in the sky who keeps a balance sheet and distributes blessing or curse according to our merit. It leaves us with the mistaken notion that life is eminently fair, that bad things happen to bad people and good things happen to good people, the illusion that our outcome is all in our hands, that we have, or can have, control over the chaos, that we can protect ourselves. "So change," it says, "and bad things won't happen to you. God will keep you safe."

What Jesus seems to have in mind is something a little less neat but much more honest, something more respectful of the mystery that surrounds us, the mystery of sorrow as well as joy, of evil as well as good. It is the mystery that Isaiah faced in the God whose thoughts are beyond our thoughts, whose ways are not our ways. Jesus refuses to bolster the illusion that we protect ourselves by good and faithful living. He refuses to give the impression that faith or morality is like an amulet that protects us or a ticket to a safe, pain-free life. He refuses to suggest that faith or good and upright living somehow make us immune to tragedy. Jesus will have none of that illusion; he dismisses that assumption by ignoring their question.

What Jesus does do is recognize his inquirers' vulnerability, their feeling of being small and fragile, which comes from their fear and sorrow. He recognizes the shudder brought on by the awareness that they are not in control and cannot guarantee their own well-being. He responds to their vulnerability by questioning them, just as every tragedy questions us.

One of the things that makes a falling tower, a crashing bus, a sudden illness, accident, or unexplained death so shattering is that it gives us each a glimpse of our own mortality, a glimpse of how fragile we are, how precarious our days, how tentative and brief our lives. Jesus uses that glimpse as an occasion for something good. He asks, "Knowing how short your life is, are you living it well? Knowing how fragile you are, where do you stand with God?" He says to repent and turn the occasion into a new beginning, a deeper walk with God, and a life more wisely and more fully lived.

One of my favorite days in the church year is Ash Wednesday, not because it's a grand celebration, but because it really does force me each year to look at the truth of myself that I so often run from or hide from or bury beneath a load of pettiness. One of the psalms appropriate to that day is Psalm 103, which says: "Our lives are like grass; we flourish like flowers of the field, but the wind passes over them and they are gone." That poignant awareness of how brief our lives are is the truth. It's not a pleasant truth, but it is an important truth, the truth Jesus was getting at and offering back as the occasion for good news, the truth that's at the heart of what Lent is all about—this season that begins on Ash Wednesday with the words, "Remember you are dust and to dust you return."

The point of such remembering isn't to depress ourselves or to shatter our confidence or to wallow in morbidity; it's certainly not to raise our level of anxiety. The point is that in remembering we may catch a glimpse of just how precious and irreplaceable are the gifts of our lives, and we may be questioned at the very heart of ourselves, much as Jesus questioned those who came to him. We may be questioned at the very core of our living about what really matters, about what we really feel, think, want, and believe, about what our priorities are and whether we live them.

Am I living a life that is good and worthwhile? Do I squander my time? Do I take my days for granted? What in them do I take for granted? Whom? Do I take time to love, to listen, to share myself? Do I waste my days in bitterness or grudges or envy? Do I embrace the day as the gift it is; do I look for its grace, its beauty, its opportunities, its delight? Do I kill my days with pettiness or busyness or fretting over tomorrow? Do I experience each day in its fullness, in all its miracle, in all its wonder? Am I open to God's presence, to God's call? Do I give myself to what really matters?

You know the kinds of questions. We all ask them—or rather are asked them—at one time or another, though more often than not we run from them in panic and fear when they appear. Jesus hands them back to us, hands us the opportunity, however difficult, to look honestly at ourselves and turn, if need be, to walk a new path with God.

Jesus' inquirers came asking, "Why?" Jesus said, "Repent," turning the question on them, turning them from their futile queries and safe, small answers to really important, weighty questions—what were they doing with their lives, and where did they stand with God? Likewise, when we ask why, Jesus' does the same for us. He reminds us that "to dust we will return" and offers us a chance to turn and find new life. He asks if our lives are well-lived and lived in God; are they lived deeply, fully, lovingly, meaningfully? May God give us the heart to face such questions and to wrestle honestly with them. As we do, may God's grace birth something new, something holy, in us.

Fourth Sunday in Lent

Joshua 5:9–12   *Luke 15:1–3,11b–32*
2 Corinthians 5:16–21   *Psalm 32*

CALL TO WORSHIP

Leader: In the great grace of God, welcome.

People: God's peace be yours.

Leader: We continue on our Lenten journey,
          a journey that will take us to the cross
          and to the empty tomb beyond.

**People: We will wade into the mystery of dying
          and of rising with new life.**

Leader: Today we will hear of a prodigal God,
          of love generous, extravagant, abandoned.

**People: We will learn of grace wide enough to embrace
          the failed and successful alike,
          the wayward and the stalwart,
          the humbled and the hardened.**

Leader: We will try to look through God's eyes
          and see the world in new perspective.

**People: We will lay aside our habits of
          ranking and judging and finger-pointing
          and let compassion be our lens.**

Leader: But will the eyes of love change everything?

People: Will there truly be a new creation?

Leader: We pray there will be,
          that the world will take on new life,
          beginning with us.

**People: Plant our hearts in you, O God.
          Grow us in your prodigal love,
          a love without boundary or limit or hesitation,
          a love joyous and free,
          in Christ. Amen.**

CENTERING PRAYER

We come, O God, to wait for you,
    to be found by you, to be touched by you.
So move among us.
Like a mother sweeps her children into her arms
    or a father holds them with a strong embrace,
    so claim us in your love.
You who runs to embrace the wayward,
    gather us when we have strayed
    from our heart's truest course.
You who lifts the fallen to a privileged place,
    raise us to our true nobility
    from whatever depths we sink to.
You who hosts a party to celebrate your family reunited,
    grant us the joy of coming home—
    to you, to ourselves.
You who meets the strong and dutiful
    with a gentle reminder of compassion,
    soften us when we grow hardened
    and make room in our hearts for others to live there.
You who lavishes love on your creation
    day in and day out,
    open our eyes and hearts to be loved
    and to love like you,
    in Christ. Amen.

CLOSING PRAYER

You who sees us through the eyes of extravagant love,
    we praise you,
    and we pray that
    our hearts may grow as large,
    our spirits as generous,
    our welcome as wide
    as yours,
in Christ. Amen.

PRAYER OF THE DAY

You whose grace is so amazing,
  we praise your name.
You give birth to a universe vast beyond imagining
  and breathe into it the wonder of life.
You give rise to species beyond counting and sustain them,
  from the one-celled amoeba to the great blue whale.
You spread people across your earth,
  rich in their diversity
  of gender and race, of culture and creed,
  of ability and limitation,
  of size and faith and shape.
You whose grace is so amazing,
  we praise your name,
  even as we pray for your healing work among us.
Where we have left you and wandered far,
  where we have taken what is yours and squandered it,
  where we have settled for work that diminishes us,
  body, spirit, or community,
  bring us to our senses and call us home.
Where we have remained with you in name but not in spirit,
  where we drive our faith as a wedge between us and others
  or use it as a weapon to judge, demean, or exclude,
  where we have grown calculating in our ways,
  with an eye only toward what we will get out of things,
  crack us open and call us to your party.
Where we have forgotten our kinship with one another
  and with all your earth,
  raise us from our walking death into life indeed.
Be with all those who have been forgotten or neglected.
Be with all who live in the shadows of poverty
  or brutality or deep, deep sorrow.
Be with all who have fallen prey to despair,
  to abuse, to addictions.
You whose grace is so amazing,
  work the wonder of new life
  where life has grown wretched.
Seek out the lost that they may be found,
  the blind that they may see,
  the dead that they may live anew in you.
You whose grace is so amazing,
  we praise your name. Amen.

CHILDREN'S SERMON

Who has ever been angry with your brother or sister? Who has ever been angry with your mom or dad? Who has ever felt angry or left out because your mom or dad did something nice for your brother or sister or someone else that they didn't do for you, or because they treated your brother or sister or someone else better than you?

We all feel that way sometimes—left out, angry. And there's nothing wrong with feeling like that.

In fact, Jesus told the story of a brother who felt that way. His younger brother took some of the family money and left home, breaking their father's heart, but he stayed home, near his father, and worked with him. One day when he was coming home from work, he heard a party, and when he asked what was going on, he found out that his brother had come home and that his father had been so happy he had thrown a party.

Do you know what the older brother did? He sat down and pouted. "My father never threw a party for me," he said to himself.

His father came out and said, "Just because I'm happy your brother is home doesn't mean I don't love you. I've always loved you and always will."

Jesus said that the father in his story is like God, who loves every single one of us. That father is like God, who loves us not because we're good or we stay near or we do the right things, but who loves us no matter what. Jesus said that father is like God, whose heart breaks when we wander away, who leaps for joy when we return, who is glad all the time we're near. Jesus said that father is like God, who always has loved us and always will, loves me and you—no matter what!

SERMON MATERIAL (2 Corinthians 5:16–21; Luke 15:1–3,11b–32)

Main Point: Paul says we no longer regard anyone from a "human point of view," a point of view which involves ranking, judging, excluding, and throwing away. In Christ we are one and live in a new creation where all have worth.

Robert Coles is a psychiatrist who has taught at Harvard and has been the leading expert on the moral life of children. He spent his career trying to understand how children grow up with a sense of justice, compassion, concern for the poor, and a willingness to give themselves to others or for what is right. A friend told me a story about him; I can't swear it's true, but it certainly has truth in it.

When in graduate school, Robert Coles went to interview Dorothy Day. If you don't remember her, she was the founder of the Catholic Workers' Movement, an outspoken advocate for economic justice and for the rights of the poor. She was a dedicated activist who lived and worked with the poor of New York City. Coles went to interview her at one of the group homes she ran in New York, a halfway house where poor men could get back on their feet. Coles was incredibly excited about meeting Dorothy Day, and when a man in clean but tattered clothing answered the door, Coles explained who he was and what he was doing there. The man told him he could find Dorothy Day in the kitchen, so Coles practically raced down the hall to find her. When he did, she was at the sink doing dishes with a man who was also clean but somewhat frayed, obviously a resident of the house. One was washing, one drying. As Coles burst into the kitchen, he blurted out, "I am so happy to be here. I have waited so long to meet you." At that point, Dorothy calmly turned to him and asked, "Which one of us do you mean?"

I'm told that Robert Coles still retells that story, and when he does he always admits that in that one moment, in the kitchen of a somewhat rundown house in a poor section of New York City, from a woman with no advanced degrees and no money to her name, he learned more about clinical style, about how to treat people with dignity, than he did in years of Ivy League graduate training.

As I said, I don't know whether the story is true, but I do know it has truth in it, not necessarily about clinical style, but certainly about living in Christ. Hear again the way Paul put it: "From now on, therefore, we regard no one from a human point of view; even though we once knew Christ from a human point of view, we know him no longer in that way. So if anyone is in Christ, there is a new creation: everything old has passed away; see, everything has become new!"

You see, if you and I had gone bounding into that kitchen, we would have seen pretty much what Robert Coles saw. There is the great, noble heroine and a nameless homeless fellow, someone who matters and someone who doesn't. For the most part, we would have talked to Dorothy Day as if the man weren't even there. That's because we generally regard things from what Paul calls "a human point of view," one that divides people into different categories and ranks them from less deserving to more deserving, from lower value to higher value, from lesser importance to greater importance. The criteria we use to categorize people vary. Their accomplishments—whether they are winners or losers; their morality—whether they are good or bad; their economic status—whether they are rich or poor; their appearance—whether they are beautiful or ugly; their education or IQ—whether they are smart or not so smart; their drive—whether they are hardworking or lazy; even their similarity to us—whether they are "ours" in terms of color, faith, family, or country. The criteria vary, but they all share the same point of view—that some people matter and some don't, that some people should get our attention, respect, help, and concern, and some shouldn't.

That's the point of view Paul tells the Corinthians to have nothing to do with. Because of Christ, we see people and things differently. Once we regarded Christ from that old point of view, and recall exactly what happened when we did. We tossed him out, nailed him up, and threw him away. But God raised him up so we would learn that with God there are no throwaways; there are no people who do not matter; there are no people who do not deserve our attention, respect, help, and concern. There are no people outside the circle of love, not God's, not ours.

That point of view, that need to regard differently, is at the heart of Jesus' parable recorded in Luke. This story of grace that welcomes home a wayward son is one of the most familiar, most loved stories in all of Scripture, and for any of us who have known shame or failure or times of moral breakdown, it is a powerful picture of God's unconditional love for us. A party is thrown for the son who comes home!

But the heart of the story is in the second half. Remember, the story is told to the people of the strictest morality who want to preserve strong values, told to those whose sense of uprightness kept away others, told to those whose faith would have nothing to do with those who were not as upright as they. They complain that Jesus eats with sinners and outcasts, those who had fallen through the cracks and ended up at the bottom of the heap. So Jesus tells them this parable, which leads up to the moment when the gracious father says to the judgmental elder brother, "This, your brother, was dead and is alive!" The father reminds the older brother to look at the younger brother differently, to look through the eyes of family, the eyes of belonging, the eyes of deep connection.

The father is telling his eldest son to regard differently the brother he's now ready to condemn, and Jesus is telling those upright folks to regard differently the so-called riffraff they so readily throw away. Paul is telling the Corinthians to regard differently each other whom they dismiss, and Dorothy Day was gently telling Robert Coles to regard differently those he overlooked. And finally, you and I need to regard differently the people we usually don't even notice at all or notice only through the eyes of our preconceptions.

For instance, the economy has been on a roll for a while, and there has been much talk about how healthy it is. Yet how do you judge that health? By the GNP? By the performance of the stock market? By the bond market? By corporate bottom lines? By how well your investments are doing? All of those measures are included in what Paul meant by "a human point of view," because they don't notice somebody—the one in five children in certain parts of the country and one in three adults who do not get to eat three meals a day because they cannot afford it.

The Bible uses a different measure for the health of a society, for the health of an economy or nation. If you want to know how healthy a society is, look at how the least, the worst off, are treated—the poor, the widow and orphan, the stranger. Over and over and over again the Bible lifts up that measure of health. Why? To sting people with guilt? To throw a wrench in the works? To be a stick in the mud? Or rather, to invite us to see those we normally don't see and to see them through the eyes of family, to see that they belong to us, to see them as people who matter.

Imagine that! Imagine if we were to see value in those we never noticed, to see them as belonging instead of as different. How would it affect our feelings about welfare, about guaranteed health care, about the minimum wage? Imagine. How would it affect the whole atmosphere of violence against homosexuals, the angry and judgmental exclusion, if we were to regard differently, through the eyes of connection, the eyes of a "we" that embraces rather than divides, through eyes that cherish and welcome with open arms? Imagine. How would it affect our deep racial tensions, our estrangement, the walls of anger and indifference we build against each other, if we were to look through the eyes of family, of belonging? Imagine.

How would it affect our lifestyles, our pursuits, the things we buy, what we keep, what we give? How would others be affected if we looked with different eyes across the globe at the dire poverty of so many, eyes that shut to no one, eyes that throw none away, eyes that see none as expendable, eyes that see each as if he or she mattered? Imagine.

The story of a father, gracious, generous in love, invites us to look with such eyes. This Jesus, radical in his welcome of others, invites us to look with such eyes. Paul invites us to look with them. The gentle humility of Dorothy Day invites us to look with them. They all invite us to look with different eyes, to regard no longer from a human point of view, but from the point of view that is ours in Christ—a point of view in which we all matter, really; in which we belong to one another. They invite us to look through such eyes, eyes like God's.

What difference would it make if we were to see as Jesus invites us to see? I can't say. I don't know what would happen if we did. I suspect there might be a new creation—not just in the looking, but in lives made new, loved shared, hope given birth. Imagine that! It's our birthright in Christ to do so.

"From now on, therefore, we regard no one from a human point of view; even though we once knew Christ from a human point of view, we know him no longer in that way. So if anyone is in Christ, there is a new creation: everything old has passed away; see, everything has become new!" Brothers, sisters, let's open the eyes that are ours in Christ.

Fifth Sunday in Lent

Isaiah 43:16–21   *John 12:1–8*
Philippians 3:4b–14   *Psalm 126*

CALL TO WORSHIP

Leader: In the great grace of God, welcome.

People: God's peace be yours.

Leader: We continue on our Lenten journey,
a journey that will take us to the cross
and to the empty tomb beyond.

**People: We will wade into the mystery of dying
and of rising with new life.**

Leader: Today we will look at time's relentless movement,

People: a great tide sweeping everything along.

Leader: The worst comes to an end,

**People: but so, too, does the best–
crumbles, washes away.**

Leader: Though we dig in our heels
and cling for all we are worth,
our fingers are pried loose.

People: Our grip is broken, and on we move . . .

Leader: only to discover that God is at work,
opening a way.

**People: Can it be that the ashes of yesterday
are God's fertile soil?**

Leader: Only to discover that God continues to create.

People: Can it be that God works new life?

Leader: We pray it is so,
pray for God's wonder among us.

**People: Plant our hearts in you, O God.
Grow in us a hope
as sure as your creative touch.
Grow our lives into promises
of your healing ways,
in Christ. Amen.**

CENTERING PRAYER

Mighty God,

    in Jesus of Nazareth you traveled empty-handed

    through a brief life

    to invite us to be free.

Yet we who follow you are so weighed down

    that we can barely travel at all.

We carry the wounds of yesterday

    like weights on our souls,

    our failures like anchors holding us fast.

We carry the dashed dreams and disappointments,

    the slights and angers of long ago,

    like so much heavy luggage.

Our dreams fulfilled and great accomplishments

    we pack like trophies we cannot give up,

    and our spirits are so wrapped around things

    that they are not free to move.

But yours, O God, is the great expanse of yet-to-come,

    the gracious frontier of what is unfolding.

We know you most surely when we lean forward in hope,

    when we travel into your new day.

Touch us, O God, and ready us to journey with you.

Lighten our step.

Lighten our hearts.

Lighten our loads.

Loosen the grip of all that holds us in place

    and all we are afraid to lose.

Free us to leave fear behind

    and to follow you boldly,

    in Christ. Amen.

CLOSING PRAYER

Creative God,

    your Spirit is ever before us, fashioning a way,

    ever behind us, prodding us on,

    ever within us as new life unfolding.

We praise you,

    and we pray for eyes to see, hearts to welcome,

    lives to embrace,

    the new work of your hands,

    in Christ. Amen.

PRAYER OF THE DAY

With all that is within us, O God, we bless your holy name!
You who swaddle earth in the glory of the night sky,
 you who paint sunrise and sunset like a master artist,
 you who sing with many and varied voices,
 the bullfrog, the lark, the alley cat, and stray dog,
 the whale, coyote, loon, and child,
 we praise you.
You who unfold each dawn, a bold new beginning,
 you who pour grace into each day
 from the trilling of the morning bird
 to the droning of the nighttime locust,
 you who breathe life into us afresh each day,
 we praise you.
You who filled yesterday with enough richness to satisfy our souls,
 you who fill today with life and laughter and love enough to keep us going,
 you who will fill tomorrow with the wealth of your presence,
 we praise you.
This day, and each day, open our eyes to see and our hearts to savor
 the wonder and abundance of your grace.
Shape in us spirits ready to receive the gifts you give
 and to await what comes next.
We pray for those who know you most as absence—
 those who are tortured each day, within and without;
 those who know the chronic ache of a shattered heart,
 a broken home, a crumbled community;
 those whose hope has been nibbled away by poverty
 or disease or the slow passing of time;
 those who know terror or shame or grief.
You who open a way,
 give them drink in their desert and sustain them;
 give them grace in abundance
 that the seeds of their tears may yield crops of joy.
You who give each day, give them this new day—and us all—
 that it may be filled with praise of you.
Alleluia, O God of life! Amen.

CHILDREN'S SERMON

Have with you pictures of a time that was very good for you—a special trip, an ordinary vacation, a party, a time that you enjoyed a great deal. Pass the pictures and tell the children briefly what was going on, what made that time great. Be sure to say how much fun it was and how hard it was to have that time end.

Have you ever been somewhere special or done something special or just had a time so good that you never wanted it to end? That you wanted it to go on forever? A time so good you knew nothing could ever be better?

Give the children time to answer, to talk a little about those times.

Isn't it hard to have those times end, to go home again, to know things just won't be that good tomorrow?

Well, let me tell you something. There's a trick to making it easier, a trick Isaiah taught a long time ago. Isaiah was speaking to people who were sure that things could never be better than they were a long time before that, that God had made things the best they could be a long time ago, and they'd never be that good again. So Isaiah told them, "Stop. Look now. God is doing something good today."

That's still good advice for all of us today. Stop! Look now! See today what's good that God is giving—air to breathe, friends and family to love, food, a chance to help someone, time to play, to enjoy, so much good.

The best isn't over. God keeps giving. All we have to do is remember the trick: Stop! Look! See today the good God is giving.

SERMON MATERIAL (Isaiah 43:16–21; includes Philippians 3:4b–14 and John 12:1–8)

Main Point: Today's Scripture passages all point to a faith that knows how to let go of the past, not only the wounds but the triumphs as well, and to journey on with the God who was with us yesterday and will be with us tomorrow.

My memory strikes me as somewhat strange, something like a big closet in my head that is stuffed full of things, many of which have no particular importance, crammed in no particular order. Every now and then it is as if the door swings open and something spills out for no apparent reason.

One recent memory that spilled out was of the first time my oldest son went to a beach. Here this little fellow stood before the immense ocean, and he was thrilled. He stood by the edge, just taking it all in, when he noticed that the waves swirling around his feet were causing him to sink. He pulled his feet out of the sand that was now covering them and replanted them on top of the sand, turning back to watch the water, only to discover that he was again sinking. Once again he pulled his feet out and planted them firmly. Then he crossed his arms and glared at the ocean as if he could stare it into submission.

That memory tumbled out recently for no apparent reason, but it strikes me as an apt metaphor for the way so many of us do so much of our living. We plant our feet in time, only to discover that time, like the ocean, is constantly moving, swirling, eroding the ground on which we stand, grinding, flattening, changing it, which is not such a bad thing when things themselves are bad; it's nice then to know they'll change. But that truth is tougher to take when we consider that time may take away the good things as well. So we do our best to plant our feet firmly and stare time down, to hold it at bay, to hang on to "now" or "then." Among other things, we have tummy tucks, face-lifts, hair transplants, wrinkle removers, and hair dye, and with all of them, the wash of time still moves as relentlessly as the waves; the sand under our feet shifts, and we still age, our broad mind and narrow waist changing places. We are not so young as we once were nor as young as we wish we still could be, no matter how firmly we planted our feet or how fast we stood with defiance.

It's not only people who try to hold time still. Institutions too, especially churches, try to hang on to the past long after it is past. We live as if what we once believed is what we must always believe or what we once did is what we must always do, and we fight tooth and nail against any changes. That leads to the kind of foolishness that condemned Galileo because he dared to say the sun doesn't revolve around the earth or to the silliness like that of a church I know. Years ago in a time when our culture was much different, a special annual worship service was begun there for women at eleven o'clock on a Wednesday morning. Today the majority of the women in that congregation are employed outside of the home and are incapable of attending on a Wednesday morning. Only a handful are ever present anymore, but the congregation has yet to respond to the change in circumstances of its members. Though the matter has been discussed, they have kept the "sacred" time because "that is when it has always been!" The service for women is held when women cannot come, as the church tries to stare down change.

We cling to beliefs, practices, and even things in the church, especially buildings. An urban church, once thriving but now struggling in a changed neighborhood, its building showing signs of wear, applied for two grants from two very different foundations. One foundation was interested in the preservation of historic church buildings and awarded money for the upkeep and restoration of church buildings; the other was interested in community development and awarded money to groups, including churches, that had vital programs to meet the social needs of the community. The church was offered both grants that it applied for, but there was a problem. The historic foundation awarded the money with the proviso that no changes be made to the church structure, while the community development foundation awarded the money, which was for a soup kitchen and food/clothing program geared toward helping people back into the job market, with the proviso that some changes be made to the building. The church had to choose between the money to restore its once grand building and the money to make a difference in the lives of people now in its community. They chose the building, staring down time and deciding, in effect, that the church should be a museum rather than an operating kiln in which faith and life and community are forged

Whether we look at ourselves individually or together, there are lots of ways we plant our feet and stare down time, as if we really could hold it off, as if it would be a good thing if we could hold it off, as if the movement of time and the changes it works were nothing but our enemies.

It's there that Scripture has something surprising to say, at least to those whose faith is tied up in clinging to some past or preserving some bulwark or defending some solid place to stand. The Scripture as a whole, and especially our passages for today, offer us a God who is not tied down to the past, a God who is not particularly concerned about preserving the past, a God who is at work creating something new and inviting us to come along.

Hear Isaiah say it: "Remember not the former things, nor consider the things of old; behold, I am doing a new thing," which makes perfect sense given that the people he is speaking to want to forget their recent past, a past of suffering and humiliation. The people of Israel have been exiled, carted away from their homes, their city destroyed and their land made desolate. They would love to forget all that, except that's not what Isaiah has in mind. What he talks about forgetting are the good things, which for Israel are the parting of the sea, their exodus from Egypt, the overthrow of their enemies. Forget it all, Isaiah tells them, for God is doing something new. Let go and turn toward the work God is doing now.

Paul tells the Philippians pretty much the same thing. Hear him. "Forgetting what lies behind and straining forward to what lies ahead," he writes, "I press on toward the goal of the upward call of God in Jesus Christ. . . ." "Forgetting what lies behind and straining forward to what lies ahead" makes perfect sense as a way of overcoming the shortcomings of the past or rising above the sorrows and failures of yesterday. But that's not what Paul is writing about. He is talking about leaving the best achievements and greatest accomplishments behind, like his own, which he lists right before saying it is time to forget what lies behind. He includes his lineage from the highest caliber of people, the best education, the most faithful piety, and an absolutely blameless moral life. That's the past Paul wants to leave behind! Why? Because God moves on, God creates, God has more in store, and above all else, Paul wants to live in tune with God, the same God who made yesterday so good in the first place.

What Isaiah and Paul are both pointing to is a faith that doesn't see the passing of time as an enemy, that needn't plant its feet and stare down or defy change, a faith that has more interest in what God is doing now and will yet do than in what God did yesterday. They are both pointing to a God who hasn't finished yet, a God who is still at work moving us. They are pointing to a faith willing to move on with God; a faith that knows that, however painful it is to leave the past behind, God holds something in store ahead; a faith that trusts God to remain with us and to lead us on to new blessings, new challenges, new tasks. They are pointing to a faith that believes God continues to create, in our lives and our world, a faith confident of God's goodness and trusting God's continuing work, a faith "straining forward to what lies ahead," knowing that God is at work there.

Now be careful. What neither Isaiah nor Paul is doing is discounting the past; they don't dismiss yesterday as meaningless. It is always important to acknowledge what has been good and rich and meaningful in the past, since we will only have eyes to see where God is going and hearts willing to trust if we recognize that God has been with us before. It's also important to recognize how our lives have wrapped themselves around what has been good in them, because we can't move on while our lives are still wrapped around what is no longer moving.

Significantly, the gospel lifts up as important Mary's act of grief, her anointing of Jesus with burial perfume, as more important even than caring for the poor. Why? Because we can't be open to what God is doing or where God is calling us if our eyes and hearts are anchored, stuck, still looking behind us. It's crucial to allow ourselves to say good-bye, as Mary does, to give ourselves permission to let go, to grieve what was once good and is no longer. It took a long time and much work to wrap our lives around something or someone; it will take time and work to unwrap them too.

And it will take the kind of faith Paul and Isaiah are pointing to, a faith convinced that God is leading somewhere new, creating something new, something good and holy, a faith willing to move on with God.

I once knew a woman with that kind of faith, a woman in her eighties when I met her and visited her regularly in the nursing home where she was staying. Shortly before I met her she had had to pack up everything and give away most of it, had to leave her lifelong home and friends in order to move across the state to be in a nursing home near her daughter. Her husband was ailing when I met her, all but completely incommunicative, and she herself was hard of hearing, practically blind, and confined to a wheelchair. If anyone had a reason to live in yesterday, to spend her time in memory, to plant her feet firmly in the past and stave off change, it was this woman. Yet as I visited her, she told me very little about the past. She told me about the kindness of some of the staff at the home and of visits from her daughter. She told me of the squirrels that played outside her window and the bus trip from the home to the mall. She told me about another woman at the home who was going through some turmoil and how she befriended that woman, listened to her, and tried to care for her. She told me small bits of her life but very little of the past. Then one day she told me that when she first arrived at the home she spent a great deal of time remembering, remembering the friends she had just left, remembering her life, remembering all the way back to her days as a schoolgirl. Remembering is all she did—until one morning she awoke and realized that it was time to stop that and move on. "I have to look for what God has in store today!" she said.

That's the faith that Paul and Isaiah are pointing to, a faith that knows that God keeps working, that knows God is a God of miracles, of healing, of a new day; a faith that knows that whatever comes God will be in it with us, working something good; a faith that knows how to lean forward and trust God's touch to open a way. That's a faith that doesn't have to plant its feet and stare down the ocean; it has learned to ride the waves of God's creative love.

May something of that faith grow in us; may we learn how to lean forward in trust and to move on with God.

Palm Sunday / Passion Sunday

Isaiah 50:4–9a
Philippians 2:5–11
Psalm 31:9–15

Luke 19:29–42 (Story of the Palms)
Luke 22:14–23:56 (Story of the Passion)

INTRODUCTION TO THE SERVICE

Given changes in work, family, and devotion, many of which the church has had little say in, Good Friday in many places has been waning in importance as a day of worship. In its absence, however, people move from the "Hosannas" of Palm Sunday to the "Alleluias" of Easter Sunday without ever experiencing the shouts of "crucify," the sounds of nails, and the final sigh in between. This raises the danger that the gospel will appear as the promise of good times and happy smiles rather than one of new life raised from the depth of tragedy, brutality, horror, and pain.

To be sure that resurrection is experienced as God's response to crucifixion, new life as God's answer to horror and brutality, lectionaries name this day "Palm and Passion Sunday" and include as the Gospel reading the entire Passion story, from the meal on Thursday night to the burial on Friday afternoon. In each of the Gospels, that is a rather long selection, one difficult to follow when read beginning to end by one voice. If the entire Passion story is to be read, finding ways to make it more listenable is important. Smaller sections, each read by a different voice; readings interwoven with choral selections and/or hymns; or a dramatic reading by a group of people are all ways of cutting the tedium of one long reading. Appropriate sensory material (shouts of "Crucify!" or the banging of nails into wood) also help to draw attention into the story.

The entry into Jerusalem (the Palm Sunday text) can be used in addition or instead of the entire Passion story. Again, action or materials appropriate to the story (waving palms, strewing palms in the aisles, procession into or around the sanctuary by the whole congregation or some specific representatives) all help to give flesh to the story so that it meets us on more levels than merely the verbal.

The following resources weave together images from both the entry into Jerusalem and the Passion. Some of these materials would also be appropriate for a Good Friday service.

CALL TO WORSHIP

Leader: We gather to remember

People: and to worship the Christ of God.

Leader: You who comes humbly among us,

People: we praise your name.

Leader: You who rides on a donkey
             like a prince of peace,

People: we greet you with palms.

Leader: You whom crowds welcome with loud cheers,

People: we shout, "Alleluia!"

Leader: You who brings with you
             those we'd rather ignore,

People: we often deny we know you.

Leader: You who calls us to love
             regardless of the risk,

People: too frequently we betray you.

Leader: You who demands that we change our ways,

**People: our joyous welcome easily turns to
             shouts of "Crucify!"**

Leader: You who reveals who we are,

**People: we pray your grace
             to shape what we will be.
             Make us yours
             that we may love like you
             and shout your praise:
             Alleluia! Alleluia!**

CENTERING PRAYER

We praise you, O God,
    with waving palms
    and joyous songs
    and shouts of "Alleluia!"
But as long ago shouts of welcome
    turned to cries of "Crucify!"
    we know our praise can be muted
    by lives that fail to honor you.
So this day claim us.
Call forth from us not only praise,
    but hearts made new in your love,
in Christ. Amen.

BLESSING OF THE PALMS

Leader: God is with you.

People: And also with you.

Leader: Let us give thanks to God.

People: It is right to give God thanks and praise.

Leader: It is right and good, O God, to praise you always.
               This day we remember that Jesus entered Jerusalem.

People: Hosanna in the highest!

Leader: He was greeted by those who spread palm branches
               and cloaks along the way.

People: Hosanna in the highest!

Leader: They honored him as your Chosen One, crying,
               "Blessed is the one who comes in the name of the Lord!"

People: Hosanna in the highest!

Leader: May the palms we raise be signs that we welcome your Christ.

**People: May our lives be shaped by Christ's way of love;
        may our hearts be filled with praise of you. Amen.**

CLOSING PRAYER

Through the great grace that empties itself for us,
    refresh us, O God.
By the great love that will bear even a cross,
    claim us, O God.
With the mighty love that turns defeat into victory,
    free us, O God.
In daring love that does not count the cost,
    mold us, O God, until we are yours,
in Christ. Amen.

PRAYER OF THE DAY

Living Christ,
    you have brought us again to this holiest of weeks,
    when you claim us for your own.
Be with us as we walk through it, that we might never again be the same.
You who entered the holy city to speak truth to "the powers that be,"
    teach us not to be intimidated by those mightier than we,
    but to speak truth and to confront the things that are not right.
You who came riding humbly on a donkey,
    not to threaten others or to win over them,
    but to win them over by your mighty vision,
    teach us the power of a disarmed life and the magnetism of a life well lived.

You who wept for those who did not know the things that make for peace,
     teach us to weep where there is no peace, and tutor us in the ways to build it.
You who were greeted by cheers that before long turned to bloodthirsty cries,
     teach us steadiness of purpose and strength of heart
     despite shifting winds around us.
You whose anger flared when injustice masqueraded as God's way,
     teach us the fire of holy indignation, of passionate faith and rage for justice.
You who ate at table with those who would fail, betray, deny, abandon you,
     teach us to love without condition.
You who were mocked, beaten, and judged but still forgave those who abused you,
     teach us how to forgive, how to return blessing, not curse.
You who commended your spirit to God and breathed your last,
     teach us how to let go, how to lean into God with all we are and to trust.
You who died, innocent of all crime, the victim of others' hatred and fear,
     turn us from all hatred and from the fear that keeps us apart.
Help us to learn from you to love.
Living Christ, as we enter this Holy Week,
     be with us and touch us.
Shape us and ready us for the new life you bring
     to us and to your world.
Living Christ, make us yours. Amen.

CHILDREN'S SERMON

Have noisemakers on hand—drums, sticks, kazoos, whistles, anything with which to make a joyful noise.
Have you ever been to a parade or seen one on television? What are parades like? Are
they happy or sad, quiet or loud? What do you see at them? *Expect descriptions of things
like floats, balloons, marching bands, clowns. In our small town, no parade is complete without
soldiers and vehicles from the local National Guard center and fire engines from the surrounding
volunteer fire companies.*

The Bible tells about something like a parade on the day Jesus entered the big city of
Jerusalem. There were no soldiers in this parade; Jesus was riding a donkey to show he
wanted to win hearts not wars. A great crowd of people cheered, threw things before
him, and followed him. It was a parade to welcome Jesus, by people who wanted to
meet him, be near him, learn from him, and follow him.

So I thought we could have a parade *(pass out the noisemakers while saying the rest)*—any of
you who want to meet Jesus or be near him or learn from him or follow him. We'll have
a parade to welcome him, and all you have to do is make noise and be happy.

*Lead the children around in a stomping march, making noise and having fun. They'll have no
trouble with that. Add some shouts of "Hooray for Jesus!" When it's time to stop, just collect the
noisemakers, or if you need more control, simply yell, "Stop!" and ask them to finish with one more
cheer of "Hooray for Jesus!"*

SERMON MATERIAL *(Luke 21:14–23:56)*

Main Point: When seen in the light of the cross, our failures, our discouraged cynicism, our wounds and sorrows all take on a new appearance.

While I was in seminary I helped pastor a tiny church in a struggling working-class neighborhood in a northeastern city. Folks struggled there because their lives were blue-collar but their world was fast on its way to no longer being so, on its way to having no room for their blue-collar ways. That not only meant that they felt out of place; it meant they were in constant fear for their jobs and that they were plagued by low wages, poor schools, and growing problems with drugs and violence in their neighborhood. It was not a pretty place.

The neighborhood had several Protestant churches, all tiny, and each year they did a few things together, like a Lenten series, Good Friday services, and pulpit exchanges, so we got to know each other and to know each other's buildings. One of the churches had an interesting sanctuary. The pulpit area was raised with the pulpit in the center, and behind it was a large stained-glass window. It must have been facing east, because every time I preached there in the morning for our pulpit exchange, the sun would be shining through it. What was unusual was the shape of that window, a huge stained-glass cross that dominated the whole front of the sanctuary. I don't know whether they thought it was beautiful when they built the church or if they just thought it was important to keep our eyes on the cross, but you couldn't sit in that congregation, especially in the morning, without seeing the cross.

The window had another effect, though. When I would stand at the pulpit and look on the congregation, the window behind me, I couldn't help but see the light of the cross stretched out on them. In fact, I couldn't see them at all, couldn't see their faces, happy or careworn, couldn't see their bodies, proud or broken, joyful or sorrowing, couldn't see anything about them, except in the light of the cross.

I'll share a secret with you, something I never told them. I always thought that window was ugly. Not only was it gaudy, not only did the cross look strange in stained-glass, but the sunlight streaming through it was a sickly color, some strange mixture of blue and red that came out a horrible purplish-pink. I always thought it was ugly, and yet, through the years, I've found myself remembering it again and again, found myself yearning to stand again in that pulpit and to look out on something—some moment, some situation, some person—and to see it as I saw that congregation, to see it only in the light of the cross.

It's me, or others, I've wanted to see in that light, at times when failure has seemed so obvious, at times when I've been aware of nothing so much as my own flaws or those of someone else, at times when what is so clear is all that is in me, or in them, that is downright ugly—the darkness, the duplicity, the divided loyalties, the self-absorption, the confusion and weakness—all that is simply unlovable. When that's all I can see, I remember the window again and the light shining through, because in the light of the cross, everything looks so different.

Can you see it? On its human side, the cross is a move to silence the One who welcomed those the world called failures, moral and otherwise, who ate with them, befriended them, believed in them, who would go all the way to a cross rather than give up on them. On its divine side, that cross is a measure of just how far God will go to embrace us, to reclaim us, to hang on to us. All the ugliness in me, in you, in anyone, pales in the light of such love; the darkness in us loses its power to define us; the less-than-flattering truth about us is overwhelmed by a greater truth–about God, who will not let us go, who will not give us up, who will not stop seeing in us something worth hanging on to, who will not stop looking on us with the love we see in the light of the cross.

It's me I've wanted to see in the light of the cross, or others, at times when the cynicism in me, or them, grows strong; when I am acutely aware of just how huge are the horrors of the world and just how small I/we are; when all the violence–kids killing kids!–and hatred, the poverty and hunger and despair around us seem to dwarf whatever good we may do; when I begin to lose the faith that what we do matters or the hope that anything could be different. Why bother? What difference can I make? Can we? When that is all I can see, I remember the window again and the light shining through, because in the light of the cross it all looks so different.

Can you see it? On its human side that cross is the world's response to one trying to make a difference, a dead-end for one daring to care. On its divine side, that cross is a story of God using the bleakest of moments, the most meager of resources, the most unlikely, unpromising of tools to work something good. That's why the Gospels all respond to the cross with a cry of faith, why we decorate our sanctuaries with crosses. If God can use a cross, a vicious tool of execution, to work good, what can God do with us? All the doubts in me about what we can do pale before such a God at work among us; all the horrors of the world that look so large and seem impossible even to dent shrink in size before the One who can do so much with so little; all the discouragement and excuses in me that bottle up my caring are disarmed by One who turns a cross into glory, who uses a cross to heal, who alters the world with an afternoon's brokenness. Imagine what such a God can do at work with us in the power we see in the light of the cross.

It's me I've wanted to see in that light, or others, at times when life has reached up to kick us in the teeth, when the wind has been knocked out of us, or the life or the hope, when the bottom has fallen out of our world and all that is left is our muted "Why?" or a sorrowful tear or silent anger. It may be a spouse who leaves us, who dies, or a friend or a child; it may be the illness that invades our bodies or the burglar who invades our home; it may be the accident that robs us of the spring in our step or of our confidence. There are so many ways we can be stunned or shattered or bruised, but it's then when all seems lost, when joy becomes sorrow, when we know what it is to be defeated and to have no hope left in us. When I've been there, or been there with others, when that's all that I can see, I remember the window and the light shining through, because in the light of the cross it looks so different.

Can you see it? On its human side that cross gives us precisely what we know at times–defeat, a good man crushed, an innocent man done away with. On its divine side, that cross leans forward. On its divine side, that cross is but the first part in a two-act play. It gives us a crushing blow that is not so final, a dead-end where a way will open. It points like an arrow to Sunday and proclaims that, no matter how it looks now, all is not lost—even now God is at work, even now God is opening a way.

Ha! If the cross is not final, if even there God is not finished, then when does sorrow have the final word? When is the door closed to life, the possibility of new life gone? When does God abandon us to the aches and emptiness and tragedies that haunt us? "Never!" says that cross. "Never!" And though that doesn't take the fear out of our bellies or the sting out of our sorrow, it sustains us. It reminds us that we don't face our trials alone and that they will not have the final word. That word belongs to God, whose promise we see in the light of the cross.

It really was an ugly window, the stained-glass cross in that church. But then, as with any window, what matters is not the window itself, but the light it lets in and the world you see through it. That's why I've come back in my memory again and again through the years to that ugly stained-glass cross—to stand in its light and see the world through it, a world graced by a God who loves us no matter what, a world where God is working something holy through us, a world where, even when life fails, God remains with us and builds anew. That's a world worth seeing, a world worth giving your heart to, a world worth saying thanks for. It's our world, in the light of the cross. Thanks be to God!

Maundy Thursday

Exodus 12:1–4,(5–10),11–14   *John 13:1–7,31b–35*
2 Corinthians 11:23–26   *Psalm 116:1–2,12–19*

INTRODUCTION TO THE SERVICE

The lectionary reading focuses on the thirteenth chapter of John's Gospel and the act of Jesus stooping to wash his disciples' feet. In fact, the name of this day is derived from that chapter (Maundy, from *mandatum*, the Latin word for "command"). However, the night vibrates with so much more in Christian imagination–the bread and wine at table; Jesus' prayerful struggle in the garden; his betrayal, arrest, and abandonment. While it is appropriate to stay only with the stated text, the story in John's Gospel, it is equally appropriate, and perhaps more meaningful to some who come this day, to weave in the other vivid images associated with this night, using the Gospel of the year, Luke. The appropriate passages in Luke are: at table (22:14–34 or 38); in the garden (22:39–46); the arrest (22:47–54a).

One way to incorporate each of those images and readings is to plan a ritualized act to go with each. For the washing at table, a washing would be appropriate, certainly of feet, if the group is not too large, or the feet of representatives of the congregation; but also the washing of hands would enact touch and the use of water while posing less threat to modern congregations. Holy Communion is appropriate to the meal shared. To enact the prayerful struggle in the garden, a time of silent prayer or guided meditation, particularly one oriented to discerning and accepting God's will, would fit well. The starkness of the final image–betrayal, arrest, and abandonment–can be ritualized by doing something that leaves some visual starkness. Stripping the sanctuary, chancel, or altar of color or adornment or covering the altar or cross in black or something equally barren looking, like netting, would be appropriate.

The following resources include a prayer suitable for following each of these ritualized acts.

CALL TO WORSHIP

Leader: Come, friends, gather here.
People: We join to praise God.
Leader: What makes this night different from any other night?
People: A meal, a towel and a command, a garden, and an arrest.
Leader: A meal?
People: A sign of love even for those who betray and deny.
Leader: A towel and a command?
People: A call to love even as we are loved.

Leader:	A garden?
People:	**A time to wrestle until we can accept God's will.**
Leader:	An arrest?
People:	**Where the good is overcome**
	and the "faithful" flee into the night.
Leader:	What makes this night different from any other?
People:	**We see what is worst in us**
	and the love that holds us anyway,
	the love that calls out our best.
	May the mystery of that love renew us,
	this night and always.
	Alleluia! Alleluia!

CENTERING PRAYER

Wondrous God,
>   gather us this holy night.
Still all that distracts us from you.
Ready us for all that is about to unfold,
>   that we may meet again
>   the depths of your love for us
>   and hear again your call
>   to rise to love others,
in Christ. Amen.

PRAYER AFTER THE MEAL

God in Christ,
>   you know our failings,
>   yet you gather us at table and feed us.
For the wonder of such grace, we praise you.
For the honor of such a meal, we thank you.
For life renewed in such wanton love, we bless you
>   and give thanks that we are yours. Amen.

PRAYER AFTER THE WASHING

Christ of God,
>   you stoop as a servant to us
>   and give us a towel,
>   that we might serve others.
For your love that washes us
>   and makes us yours,
>   for your love that prods us

and sends us to others,

    we give you thanks.

Grow us in that love,

    this night and always. Amen.

PRAYER IN THE GARDEN (Prayer of the Day)

In the stillness around us this night, O God,

    we sense all that is unsettled within us—

    the concerns of this day, the irritations, the unfinished business,

    and deeper, the fears that wake us at night, the secret shame we carry,

    the pain with which we limp, the decisions we must make but cannot see how.

Be with us where we struggle.

Remain by our side so that we will not face that alone.

Strengthen us by your presence and in your love.

Grant us courage that we may be with others,

    even where we can do nothing but stand and wait,

    where we cannot understand their pain nor take it away,

    where we would rather flee than feel our helplessness.

Be with us that we may be with them,

    and by our presence, ease their lonely ache.

Be with a world that waits for peace, for justice,

    for the cries of hungry children to end,

    for the sharing of food to be more important than profits,

    for the building of a future to be more important than the amassing of assets,

    for what is good for all, especially the weakest,

    to be more important than what is wanted by the powerful.

Be with a world that waits for your shalom, your fullness of life.

Keep us hungering and thirsting, and by your presence, waiting,

    lest we settle for less.

Open us, O God, to each other's pain and to the pain of earth itself.

Help us not to run nor to turn away, but to be present to each other,

    that the bond that is forged when we are together

    might give us strength

    and be the soil in which healing grows.

In the stillness of this night, we come, O God.

Our hearts are heavy within us.

Remain with us, and grant us your peace. Amen.

PRAYER AFTER THE STRIPPING OR COVERING

Gracious Christ,

    we betray you,

    we deny you,

    we fail to wait with you,

    and we run away,

    yet you give yourself for us.

Write that wonder deep in our hearts,

    that we might know the great love

    with which you hold us

    and by which you make new our lives. Amen.

CHILDREN'S SERMON

Have with you some small paper cups, enough for each child to have one, a beverage in a large bottle or pitcher, and something to eat. Bread and grape juice would be appropriate, but the overtones of them would be of Holy Communion, and that might be a problem in congregations that do not admit non-confirmed members to communion. Also, some children will be less interested in bread and grape juice than in something a bit more to their tastes. A more kid-friendly beverage, such as apple juice, will work fine, as will something a little more kid-tasty, such as graham crackers. Distribute the cups while you talk with them.

Have you ever had to say good-bye to anyone? I don't mean a little good-bye like the ones at the end of each day, but a big good-bye to someone who was going away, someone you wouldn't see for a long time. *Give the children time to answer, and follow up with questions such as, "What did you say?" "What did you feel?" If there are no answers or no yeses, you might tell a story of a time you said good-bye.*

What do you think is important to say when you're having a good-bye like that? What do you really want the other person to know? *Give the children time to answer. You might need to lead them a little, suggesting words such as, "I will miss you," "I'll always think of you," "I love you."*

The Bible tells us of the night Jesus said good-bye to his disciples, not for good, but for the last time before everything changed for good when he was arrested and died and rose again. Jesus wouldn't be with his disciples in the same way anymore, so he said good-bye, and do you know what he did to say good-bye? He had a meal with them. He ate with them to say all those things that are important in good-byes—that he'd remember them and keep them in his heart and always love them. *Be sure to include in this list some things the children have said.*

So we're going to share a little meal too. It's not the same food, but what matters is not so much what you eat as why you eat—to remember that Jesus remembers you, that he loves you and holds you in his heart always. Let's eat!

Pour the juice into each child's cup, and let the children pass a plate of crackers. Finish by reminding them of the point of your message. We ate together to remember that Jesus remembers us, that he loves us and holds us in his heart always!

SERMON MATERIAL (Luke 22:39–46)

Main Point: As we watch Jesus agonize in the garden, we see that our own moments of anguish are not outside the life of faith; as we observe disciples who cannot watch and wait, we see our own difficulty in sharing in others' pain.

It strikes me that the garden scene Luke gives us is in some ways a mirror in which we see two reflections of ourselves. First, we see what is perhaps the most human portrayal of Jesus in all of Scripture. Here he is anguished, afraid, agonized over what is to come and wanting for all he's worth for it to be different. Luke says that Jesus is in such torment that he sweats great drops of blood!

To a lesser degree, we all have such experiences at some time or other, such as when you are alone at night, when sleep refuses to come and relieve you; when the pain in your side just won't go away, and you know it's something really serious; when the bills to be paid keep running through your mind, and you don't know how on earth you'll ever pay them; when the ache over your child and the difficulty he or she has gnaws at you, or the future you fear for them won't leave you alone; when you know you've bitten off more than you can chew and this time it's going to catch up with you, this time somebody will see you for what you really are, which is much different than anyone thinks; when you live in terror, knowing death is coming—to you, to your spouse, to someone who means as much to you as life itself.

We all know what it is to fear, to agonize, to want things to be different from what they are now or soon will be; and in Jesus, we see ourselves, see that those moments of fear and agony do not come to us alone, see that there's not something wrong with us because we have them, see that being scared or pained is not a sign that our faith is inadequate. Even Jesus wrestled, cringed, like that, which is to say, it is part of our humanity to do so, even our humanity at its best.

In Jesus we see ourselves, and we see God, meaning that this picture of Jesus' ache and tears in the dark night is meant to assure us in our dark nights. It assures us that God has been there and is there with us as we cry and tremble, that God knows and shares our ache and holds us through it. We are not alone, the Scriptures say; not even in the lonely dark night of our soul, says the garden.

It's not just Jesus in whom we see ourselves, though. A second reflection of us is in the disciples who are asked to watch and wait but instead fall fast asleep. They sleep not so much because they're tired, although they could have been. Luke says they sleep from grief, although it's not primarily the grief that soon they'll lose Jesus. They fall asleep because the task they've been given is just too difficult.

Picture it. Jesus has asked his three friends to watch and wait, but not in the sense of standing guard; Jesus has no intention of running away, so he needs no guards. It's not watching and waiting in the sense of being prepared, armed and ready; Jesus has no intention of resisting. What Jesus is asking them to do is simply to sit near him, to be with him, to stand by him as they wait for what cannot be changed.

This level of the story was opened up for me when I read Diana Eck's book *Encountering God*.[1] She tells how this story took on new meaning for her the year her young friend died during Holy Week. A small circle of friends kept up a rotation of visits at the hospital during their dying friend's last weeks, and toward the end there was nothing they could do but simply be there. Eck points out how difficult that was for her, simply to be with someone who was dying and to be able to do nothing, nothing to change it, nothing to slow it, nothing even to make it more palatable, to help her friend feel better. She could only be there, stand there, wait there, as her friend went through the dying process.

That is all we can ever do when people are troubled, grieving, dying–be there, stand with them though we can do nothing. And as we see these brave, men-of-action disciples falling asleep from the grief of having nothing to do, we see our own difficulty facing what we cannot change, what cannot be changed at all–the times when every act or word or prayer has seemed inadequate; the times when none of our cleverness or strength or determination or even our love could prevent the unfolding of what we most wanted to avoid. We see disciples who are unable to change things and unable to accept that helplessness, so they sleep, as we do, or turn on the television or read or go out for coffee or straighten up or all kinds of distractions that are the spiritual equivalent of sleep, because it is so difficult to wait, to be with, to accept what we don't want yet cannot change.

Jesus provides a hint of how to stay awake, how to accept. He prays, wrestles with God, pours out his agony, admits he wants things to be different, but then he makes room for what will not change, leaves the possibility that it may be meaningful, opens himself to trust that God will be with him through it. "Not my will, but yours," he says, embracing what he wishes, yearns, would be otherwise.

That is so foreign to our goal-oriented instinct to do something. We're taught all our lives to take the bull by the horns, to rail, connive, scheme, twist, push, work, act, do something to change things, especially undesirable things, and there is value in that, time for all that. But there is also a time to make our peace with what cannot be changed, time to wait, time to let go of our demands and trust God to be present, to work even in what we wish were otherwise. There is a time to make room for the grace of what we are helpless to change, time to relinquish our control and accept what is not ours to alter, time to say, "Not my will, but yours."

So I ask you, where in your life do you have trouble watching, waiting? Where is it difficult for you to let go, to be with someone without doing or directing? What is it in your life that you cannot change and have not yet made peace with–a loss, a person, a disappointment, a relationship, the life you thought you would have but don't? Where do you sleep because watching and waiting is too difficult?

I invite you to acknowledge that, to be with it, to invite God into it, and then simply to wait, trusting the love that fills this night despite all its chaos, trusting the love of a God who will go through anything with us and for us, trusting the love that brings peace even when all the world rages against us. I invite you to wait and know that God is with you.

1. Diana L. Eck, *Encountering God: A Spiritual Journey from Bozeman to Banaras.* Boston: Beacon Press, 1993.

Easter Sunday

Acts 10:34–43   *John 20:1–9 or Luke 24:1–12*
1 Corinthians 15:19–26   *Psalm 118:1–2,14–24*

CALL TO WORSHIP

Leader: A joyous mystery gathers us together.

People: **We come to hear again the news.**

Leader: So listen, friends:

                 The tomb that was sealed now is open.

People: **Broken is the grip of all that would box life in.**

Leader: The grave that was full now is empty.

People: **Drained is the power**
                 of all that would fill life with despair.

Leader: The One who was dead now lives again.

People: **Loose in the world**
                 is the life-renewing power of love.

Leader: God's power of new life works among us.

People: **We, too, can rise**
                 from the dark tomb of sorrow,
                 the icy hold of fear,
                 the sure death of not caring.
                 We, too, can rise to life,
                 even as praise rises within us:
                 Alleluia! Alleluia! Alleluia!

CENTERING PRAYER

You whose green thumb clothes the trees,
     whose bright palette splashes flowers with colorful life,
     whose deep symphony of life gathers an orchestra
     of trilling birds and buzzing insects
     and scampering squirrels
     to join in a song of praise:
     we raise our hearts in praise of you
     and of your life-renewing power.
You whose light ushers in the dawn,

whose touch opens the grave,
  whose wonder calls the dead back to life:
  we raise our hearts in praise of you
  and of your resurrection power.
This day we ask your holy work
  among lives still trapped in tombs.
To all in us that is broken or fearful,
  to all in our world who know only sorrow,
  in every place that has forgotten love's touch,
  give your Easter gift of new life rising.
Loose in us the power to live again,
  to hope, to dream, to laugh, to cry,
  to work, to play, to love,
  the power to treasure each passing moment
  without fear of what is to follow.
Loose in us your risen Christ,
  your love stretched out toward others,
  your laughter of life triumphant.
All praise is yours, O God. Alleluia! Amen.

CLOSING PRAYER

Wondrous God,
  we praise you for this day of new life.
Now, alive in your Spirit, send us,
  to live each day fully,
  to hope in every circumstance,
  to love without question or restraint,
  to praise you, who raises us with Christ:
  Alleluia! Amen.

PRAYER OF THE DAY

We praise you, O God.
Your faithful touch draws the light of dawn
  from the cold and dark of night.
We praise you, O God.
Your fertile touch births spring's lively miracle
  from the barren, chilly womb of winter.

We praise you, O God.

Your wondrous touch wrests new life

from the iron grip of death.

We truly praise you, O God,

even as we pray for your Easter work still in our world.

To hearts that are riddled with anxiety,

to lives that are haunted by fear,

to places that are ruled by terror,

grant your touch.

To hearts poisoned by hate,

to lives crippled by abuse,

to places marred by brutality,

grant your touch.

Where hope has died and left behind the hollow shells of people,

where hearts have learned to steel themselves against love

lest there be yet more pain,

where delight is experienced as shame or never experienced at all,

grant your touch.

Break the hold and the habits of death,

that life might rise, new and abundant,

and all the earth might join in praise.

Alleluia, great God of life. Alleluia! Amen.

CHILDREN'S SERMON

Have earplugs, ear protectors, or headphones, like those from a portable CD player, with you.

Ever see anyone wearing these? Ever try to talk to anyone wearing them? Ever feel like everybody was wearing them, like you wanted to say something and no one would listen? Ever feel like no one would listen to you because you were so young or because they just didn't care what you had to say? *Give the children time to answer.*

I have too, and we're not the first. The Bible says God gave the Easter news—that Jesus was risen—to women, and no one would listen to them. People had funny notions then that only men were important enough to listen to, but God had other ideas. God thought everyone was worth listening to, so God gave the great news to women, and God gives each of us something important to say.

God raised Jesus from the dead, and God raised all of us to be people worth listening to. So let's share the news; let's shout together, "Jesus Christ is risen! Jesus Christ is risen!" *Have the children join you in shouting the news.*

SERMON MATERIAL (Luke 24:1–12)

Main Point: In Luke's Gospel, Christ is not only risen, but he comes to those who are broken and sorrowful. Thus, Easter faith not only makes room for those who bear their own pain or that of the world; it points to the risen One who comes to share and finally heal that pain.

One year just before Easter, the father of a colleague, a woman pastor, died after a long illness. His death was difficult for the family. Despite the fact that his death was expected, they were very close, so his death took its toll. My colleague mentioned that Easter would be particularly difficult. "I don't know how I'll get through it," she said. "Everyone will expect me to be bright and perky and upbeat and joyful, and I won't have it in me. It won't be Easter in my heart."

I wonder if some of us aren't like her today. Our knees get shaky under the weight of life, our eyes brim with tears, and we just can't manage a happy smile. We try to be chipper on the outside; we put on some new clothes and an appropriate smile for Easter, but it is still Good Friday in our hearts—the innocent suffer, the good is crushed, and we can't make sense out of any of it.

I wonder if some of us aren't like my friend today. We know our share of pain, of loss, of disappointments, of demands we can barely manage, of illnesses, burdens, and heartaches. We think all the talk of Easter is nice and wish we could share it, but it is still Good Friday in our hearts.

I wonder if some of us aren't like my colleague today. We see hatred and slaughter on the news, environmental destruction, urban despair, kids killing kids, tornadoes and hurricanes ripping apart lives, and we yearn for Easter, yearn to celebrate, but we know we live in a Good Friday world.

I wonder if some of us aren't like that woman pastor today, and I wonder if the part of Luke's Gospel that is our Scripture passage for today wasn't written with those people in mind. Listen to it. The women come to the tomb and find it empty, and just when we expect shouts of joy or cries of faith, all we get is perplexity and fear. When they remember Jesus' words that he would be crucified and rise again and we're waiting for a mad dash and excited spreading of the news, all we get is a very simple, very subdued statement: they returned and told the others. When the others hear, we think we'll certainly get some cheers and shouts, some hoorays and alleluias, but what we get is disbelief; they dismiss the whole thing as delusion, women's fantasy. Even when Peter's curiosity finally gets the best of him, when he goes to the tomb and finds it empty himself, all we get is wondering.

It's all so disappointing. It's almost as if Luke has bent over backward to pull in the reins on the celebration, to settle down the joyous excitement, to dampen the party, and I wonder why. It's as if he has done his best to tone things down, cool things off, and I wonder why. It's as if he wanted to be sure we would not fill Easter day with shouting and laughing and singing, and I wonder why.

I suspect it has something to do with my colleague and those like her. I suspect Luke has too much respect for the power of Good Friday in our hearts and our world, too much respect to simply leap for joy. He has too much honesty about the chaos around us to believe faith comes quickly and easily. He knows too many people like my colleague—for whom the world is a struggle, for whom tears come more easily than smiles—to pretend that all is well. So he makes room for them in the story, room for the hesitant heart, the broken heart, the discouraged heart. He welcomes them into the story and honors their struggle and respects their sorrow, and then he dares to proclaim that Easter is for them.

Look! Look what he says! Look what comes next. Two disciples are trudging down the road to Emmaus, lost in their gloom, reeling from the collapse of their world, when a stranger joins them, walks with them, and hears their despair. When he breaks bread, they finally recognize him—risen, in their midst!

Look! The rest of Jesus' disciples are hiding in an upper room, locked away out of fear, nursing their broken hearts, lost in shame over abandoning him and in sorrow over losing him, swept away in their grief, when into their midst he comes, risen!

Look! The risen Christ comes, not to those smiling, dancing, and laughing, but to those broken and cowed, to those whose world has fallen apart. The risen Christ comes, not where all is well, but precisely where all is not well, where discouragement and sorrow and heartache hold sway. The risen Christ comes to people like Mary and Peter and even my colleague, people who know Good Friday and its power all too well. The risen Christ comes, says Luke.

This is not a promise that all is well, but rather that when all is not well, we won't have to face it alone. The risen Christ comes, which is not a promise that everything will turn out fine, but that no matter how it turns out, it cannot separate us from God or blot out God's grace. The risen Christ comes, which is not a promise that we won't walk through chaos or sorrow or even death, but that Christ will meet us in them and see us through. The risen Christ comes to touch our Good Friday lives with Easter's power, to bring some bit of life and love and hope even where we no longer believe them possible. The risen Christ comes to renew us. The risen Christ comes.

Where I live, the media has followed a story of the risen Christ coming. Over the last several years, news crews have periodically updated the story of a couple whose teenage son was beaten to death on the steps of a church as he ran from a group of boys from a different neighborhood. After his death, as blood boiled among teens in the neighborhood and the thirst for revenge was strong, his parents were very visible at teen gatherings, calling for calm, encouraging peace, turning their son's friends away from the rage they felt and their desire to continue the violence. The couple has continued to honor the death of their son by working for nonviolence among teens in several ways. In a Good Friday world, a world that reached out to crush what mattered to them, their lives have been touched by the risen Christ, as a love that will not be broken, a light of hope that has nourished others, a power of life that will not be extinguished. The risen Christ comes.

The risen Christ came to a man I know who was plagued by a midlife crisis that practically paralyzed him with a fear of dying and a sense of the meaninglessness of his life.

Nothing anymore in his life excited him or pleased him or mattered to him—not his wife, not his children, not his job, not the woodworking he had once loved so much. All of it seemed empty. There was no instant miracle for him, just a slow process, but one in which his eyes gradually opened and he looked into his same old life to see what had been hidden from him for a while—the love of his family and how rich that was, the blessing of a good job, the satisfaction of being able to create with his hands, to make beauty in his woodworking, the wonder of it all. He looked on all that had seemed so empty and gradually saw how rich and full it was. The risen Christ had come to his Good Friday heart as the strength to endure and then as a presence filling life full, renewing life, bringing a depth and joy and purpose to living. The risen Christ comes.

The risen Christ came to an ordinary man in a drug-infested neighborhood in North Philadelphia. He wanted some hope for his family, so he organized a neighborhood watch, one that kept tabs on drug dealers, cooperated with police, and pressured the whole drug trade to leave their area. He continued his work with that watch despite threats to himself and his family. He described it like this: "You live your life trying to be safe, trying to get by, to stay out of trouble's way. But at some point you have to choose between fear and what's right, between hiding away and standing up. I finally chose to stand." In a Good Friday world the risen Christ came to him as life and hope stronger than fear. The risen Christ comes.

Luke's promise this Easter to people who know the sorrow and fear and pain of Good Friday is that the risen Christ comes as love and hope and life. The risen Christ comes with a power that makes life new.

When my son was very young, he would rise with the sun and awaken me right away. This was particularly a problem as the days stretched longer and the sunrise got earlier and earlier. Hoping to get him to sleep a little later, I would make sure the shades on his windows were pulled down. Nevertheless, the sun slid underneath and managed to wake him, so I tried pulling the shades extra long, hoping to squeeze out a few more minutes of sleep. Still the sun crept in around the edges of the shades. Finally, in desperation, I tried taping his shades to the window frames, but my son pointed out the folly of what I was doing. "But, Dad," he said, "you can't keep out the light."

You can't keep out the light. That's the Easter promise. Whether it comes as a brutalized family who refuses to hate, or as a middle-aged man who finds a reason to go on, or as an ordinary person who refuses to fear—whatever face it wears, you can't keep it out. The light, the risen Christ, comes—to touch, to share, to fill our lives. In the darkness of a Good Friday world, the empty tomb whispers its promise: "You can't keep out the light."

To the chill of Good Friday hearts filled with hesitance or sorrow or fear, the empty tomb whispers its promise: "You can't keep out the light."

When our lives are held in Good Friday's grip and we know Good Friday's power, the empty tomb whispers its promise: "You can't keep out the light."

Christ is loose in the world; love's power is on the move; the risen Christ comes—to us, to you. The risen Christ comes! Alleluia! Alleluia!

AN EASTER HYMN

This hymn is metered 7.6.7.6 D and can be sung to any tune so metered, particularly Ellacombe (e.g., "Hosanna, Loud Hosanna") or Lancashire (e.g., "Lead On, O King Eternal").

The Morn Begins in Darkness

1. The morn begins in darkness
        and showered in our tears.
   Among the graves we shuffle,
        enshrouded by our fears.
   We come to put behind us
        the hope that flowered bright,
   to say good-bye to God's new dawn,
        accept the endless night.

2. But, lo, the stone is rolled away;
        now empty is the tomb.
   "He's risen!" says a stranger's voice;
        the grave's become a womb.
   Our hearts are torn by fear and hope;
        confusing is the news.
   Can we accept that God would raise
        the One the world abused?

3. A fearful silence falls on us,
        as we begin to leave.
   "The dead now lives" is just too much
        for any to believe.
   Yet back in Galilee we find,
        among us in our days,
   a life renewing all our hope
        and moving us to praise.

4. The One whom we thought shattered
        is risen from the grave.
   The love that we thought conquered
        is working still to save—
   it comes to us; it calls to us;
        its work it bids us do,
   to join in mending every wound
        until all things are new.

5. The morn began in darkness
        and showered in our tears.
Among the graves we shuffled,
        enshrouded by our fears.
We came to put behind us
        the hope that flowered bright,
but God has other plans for us—
        with dawn God breaks the night.

Section II

PRAYER DIALOGUES
AND ANTIPHONAL HYMNS

by Anne McKinstry

Dedication

To Rev. Bert Marshall
Still my pastor; always my friend

On Passion Sunday you encouraged us
to sing: "What Child Is This"

I am grateful

Introduction

This section, written by Anne McKinstry, introduces an innovative element for worship for those churches who want to add a new and creative dimension to their worship services during the Lenten season. For each of the nine services in the first section, Section Two contains both a "prayer dialogue" and a hymn. Each dialogue and hymn is designed to be read (or sung) antiphonally, with one group representing God's people (regular typeface) and the other representing God (**bold** typeface).

The prayer dialogues might also be characterized as antiphonal Scripture readings. The author has artfully woven together texts from the lectionary readings in a call-response dialogue that might be used in place of a more traditional Scripture reading.

The antiphonal hymns are based on the same scriptural themes and also crafted in a call-response format. The words are original and have been written to the tunes of familiar hymns. The tune name and well-known hymn title have been indicated for the convenience of both the congregation and instrumentalists.

Again, the regular typeface signifies the voices of God's people while the **bold** typeface signifies the voice of God. A church might divide its congregation by gender, age, or pews to achieve the antiphonal effect. Or choose one individual worship leader, pastor, or lay leader to represent God—and vary that person from week to week. You might even ask the children to be the voice of God for the reading. There is no one right way to make use of these resources.

Each reading appears on its own page to facilitate photocopying. Please feel free to reproduce as many copies of the prayer dialogues or hymns as are needed for your service.

Undo Its Heavy Chains

Isaiah 58

What is required; what sacrifice is desirable to you,
    our wonderful and righteous God?
The sacrifice that I desire is for you to loose
    the bonds of oppression; undo its heavy chains.

What is required; what sacrifice is desirable to you,
    our giving and merciful God?
The sacrifice that I desire is for you to share
    your food with the hungry; clothe the poor.

What is required; what sacrifice is desirable to you,
    our gentle and healing God?
I desire that you comfort and heal the sick.
    Call me, and hear my words: "Here I am!"

What is required; what sacrifice is desirable to you,
    our just and faithful God?
I desire that you bring the homeless into your house,
    lovingly caring for them.

What is required; what sacrifice is desirable to you,
    our gracious and forgiving God?
I desire that you hold the sinner in your forgiving arms;
    enfolding with a robe of love.

What Is Required, What Sacrifice

Isaiah 58

HYMN: "JESUS, THE VERY THOUGHT OF THEE"
TUNE: ST. AGNES

What is required; what sacrifice
    Will touch your righteousness?
Oppression grips humanity.
    Undo its heavy chain.

What is required; what sacrifice
    Will touch your mercy, love?
A hunger deep and wide prevails.
    Relieve its dreadful pain.

What is required; what sacrifice
    Will touch your healing wings?
Disease still plagues earth's happiness.
    Comfort the wounded, sick.

What is required; what sacrifice
    Will touch your faithfulness?
Affliction, homelessness persist.
    Open your hearts, your homes.

What is required; what sacrifice
    Will touch your graciousness?
Sin robs the heart of joy and peace.
    Reach out, embrace, forgive.

And Cleave to Me in Love

Psalm 91; Romans 10:8–13

We are afraid. We fear the snare of hunters.
>We fear the deadly pestilence that stalks in darkness.
>>We want to dwell in safety.

I am your refuge; call on my name.
>**No evil shall befall you when you cleave to me in love.**
>>**I am your salvation.**

We are afraid. We fear the stones, the rocks that cut our feet.
>We fear the harm of our enemies,
>>possible death and destruction.

I give my angels charge of you; they will bear you up.
>**Call on my name, and I will protect you.**
>>**Cleave to me in love.**

We are afraid. We fear temptations that we cannot overcome.
>We fear and hate the shame from the wrong that we do.
>>We need your deliverance.

I am your Savior. I will rescue you and I will honor you.
>**Cleave to me in love; then confession**
>>**will pour forth from your lips.**

We are afraid. We fear rejection; punishment for our sins.
>We fear being alone, apart from you.
>>We need your salvation.

I am Christ Jesus, a crucified and risen Savior.
>**Call my name and cleave to me in love.**
>>**Rich blessings will fall upon you.**

First Sunday in Lent

We Fear the Snare, the Pestilence

Psalm 91; Romans 10:8–13

HYMN: "HOW SWEET THE NAME OF JESUS SOUNDS"
            "IN CHRIST THERE IS NO EAST OR WEST"
TUNE: ST. PETER

We fear the snare, the pestilence
    That stalks in darkness drear.
I am your refuge; call my name,
    And cleave to me in love.

We fear the rocks, so treacherous
    That make us stumble, fall.
My angels lift you; call my name,
    And cleave to me in love.

We fear temptation's pow'rful pull
    That weakens faith and will.
I am your Savior; call my name,
    And cleave to me in love.

We fear a death, a loss of grace,
    A place apart from you.
I am Christ Jesus; call my name,
    And cleave to me in love.

Words by Anne McKinstry. From *Breathing New Life into Lent, Volume 3*, copyright 2000 by Judson Press. Used by permission.

And He Went up on the Mountain to Pray

Luke 9:28–36

Our spirits need to be refreshed. We are uninspired and weary.
> As Christ prayed on the mountain,
> we also desire a time of rest and prayer.

Come, with Christ, to the solitude of the mountain.
> **Without distractions you will hear my voice more clearly:**
> **"This is my Son, my chosen."**

Our spirits need to be revived. We are depressed and tired.
> As Peter, John, and James saw a vision,
> we also desire to see the radiance of Christ's garment.

Come, with the disciples, to the beauty of the mountain.
> **Your doubts will melt away, your faith will be stronger.**
> **Christ's holiness will be dazzling.**

Our spirits need to be renewed. We are lost, dejected, and alone.
> As Christ, and the disciples, were renewed and strengthened,
> we too desire a new spirit.

Come, with Christ and the disciples, to the strength of this mountain.
> **My message, through prophets and through Christ,**
> **will tell again of my love that lifts.**

Our spirits need to be empowered. We are unmotivated and dead.
> As disciples of Christ, we desire to hear anew his call to discipleship;
> to receive his power.

Come, with the disciples, to the power of this mountain.
> **To all my disciples I say: "Listen to him."**
> **When Christ descended, a great crowd met him.**

We Need to Climb your Mountain Height

Luke 9:28–36

HYMN: "JUST AS I AM WITHOUT ONE PLEA"
TUNE: WOODWORTH; ALSO SAXBY

We need to climb your mountain height;
>   Refresh our spirits, bask in grace.

Lifted above the day's demands,
>   **You'll hear anew my voice, so kind.**

We need to climb your mountain height;
>   Revive our spirits, bask in light.

Lifted above the clouds of doubt,
>   **You'll see anew my truth, so pure.**

We need to climb your mountain height;
>   Renew our spirits, bask in you.

Lifted above the tangled maze,
>   **You'll feel anew my strength, my love.**

We need to climb your mountain height;
>   Empow'r our spirits, bask in Christ.

Lifted above the pressing crowd,
>   **You'll heed anew his call: come, serve.**

Third Sunday in Lent
Hear, That Your Soul May Live
Isaiah 55

We hear your lavish invitation: "Come to the waters; come buy without money."
    Are we deserving of such a gift?
    Can we have a free ride?
Hearken diligently to me and drink and eat what is good;
    delight yourselves in plenty, all without price.
        Everyone who thirsts, come!

We hear your lavish desire for the earth, that rain and snow
    come down from heaven and cause seed to sprout,
        giving us bread that is nourishing.
Incline your ear to me and hear that your soul may live.
    My ways are higher than your ways.
        My thoughts are deeper than your thoughts.

We hear your lavish declarations:
    "The mountains and hills shall break forth into singing.
        Instead of the thorn shall come up the cypress."
My word goes forth from my mouth and prospers in my purpose.
    You shall go out in joy and be led forth in peace.
        Hear, that your soul may live.

We hear your lavish declarations: "Instead of the brier shall come up the myrtle.
    It shall be as a memorial,
        an everlasting sign, never to be cut off."
My word does not return to me empty, but accomplishes my purpose.
    Hear the trees clapping their hands!
        Everyone who thirsts, come to me!

Words by Anne McKinstry. From *Breathing New Life into Lent, Volume 3,* copyright 2000 by Judson Press.
Used by permission.

Your Word Is Life to Us

Isaiah 55

HYMN: "MY FAITH LOOKS UP TO THEE"
TUNE: OLIVET

Your word is life to us,
    Rain falling gently down,
    Wat'ring our lives.
Incline your ear to me;
    Hear that your soul may live,
    My ways are not your ways;
    My ways are pure.

Your word is life to us,
    Wheat blowing in the fields,
    Nour'shing our lives.
Incline your ear to me;
    Hear that your soul may live;
    My thoughts are not your thoughts;
    My thoughts are deep.

Your word is life to us,
    Cypress trees tall and straight,
    Strength'ning our lives.
Incline your ear to me;
    Hear, that your soul may live;
    You'll hear the mountains sing;
    The trees clap hands.

Your word is life to us,
    Soft myrtle rich with grace,
    Pard'ning our sin.
Incline your ear to me;
    Hear that your soul may live,
    You shall go forth in joy,
    And know my peace.

A Seeker of the Lost, the Dead

Luke 15:11–32;   *2 Corinthians 5:16–21*

Like the youth who had a fling in the city,
> we are now exhausted in body and spirit.
>> We too are disillusioned and angry. Can we come home?

Have you forgotten that I am a seeker of the lost?
> **I am like a watchful parent,**
>> **always anticipating your return.**

Like the youth who came to his senses,
> we now turn our faces and our hearts toward home.
>> Will there be yellow ribbons on all the trees?

Have you forgotten that I am a seeker of the weary and spiritually dead?
> **I am already way down the road**
>> **with the best robe to enfold you in.**

Like the youth who felt a warm parental embrace,
> we are lifted up as your love and life are breathed into our souls.
>> We are a new creation in Christ.

Come, a lavish table is spread for you.
> **I rejoice that, although you were lost, you are now found.**
>> **Life in its abundance is now yours!**

Like the youth who craved reconciliation with the parent,
> we desire a new relationship with you;
>> we want to become whole, fulfilled, and blameless.

Come, a pair of good-fitting shoes await you, replacing the worn-out pair.
> **You are now the "righteous of God,"**
>> **and given new life through Christ Jesus.**

So Lost, So Lifeless Is My Soul

Luke 15:11–32;   2 Corinthians 5:16–21

HYMN: "O, MASTER, LET ME WALK WITH THEE"
         "COME, HOLY SPIRIT, DOVE DIVINE"
TUNE: MARYTON

So lost, so lifeless is my soul;
　　I have no strength to pray to you.
Have you forgotten who I am;
　　A seeker of the lost, the dead?

I'll turn my heart from soul-less dreams,
　　Toward you, a life-filled home for me.
And I'm already down the road
　　To greet you with a welcoming hug.

Your words are life; they breathe, they lift.
　　Where is their secret; why their pow'r?
Listen again, with mind, with soul:
　　"I've come that you may have full life."

I have been brought from death to life;
　　And now my song: "Christ lives in me!"
With joyful heart, go find the lost,
　　And lift the dead to faith anew.

Words by Anne McKinstry. From *Breathing New Life into Lent, Volume 3,* copyright 2000 by Judson Press. Used by permission.

I Am Doing a New Thing

Isaiah 43:16–21;   Philippians 3:4–14

We want our faith to be alive and always new.
> We want to share, more deeply,
>> in the sufferings, death, and resurrection of Christ.

As you grow in the spirit of faithfulness,
> **You will perceive anew my words:**
>> **"I am doing a new thing"; and my grace will fill you.**

We want to pray with a deeper understanding
> and appreciation of your redemptive love.
>> We do not remember former things, only your saving grace.

As you grow in the spirit of true prayer,
> **you will know my love and my strength in your lives.**
>> **You will perceive a new thing!**

We never want to stop learning of your love for us.
> Can your gospel of salvation always be exciting and new?
> Can we always be happy?

As you grow in the spirit of humility,
> **you will hear anew the meaning of true joy and power.**
> **All things will be made new.**

We want to love, with a new vitality, our crucified and risen Lord;
> sharing, with a new intensity,
>> Christ's life, death on a cross, and resurrection.

As you grow in the spirit of gratitude,
> **the light of Christ will shine upon you.**
>> **Christ's living Spirit will be with you always.**

We Have Come to Hear Anew

Isaiah 43:16–21;   Philippians 3:4–14

HYMN: "TAKE MY LIFE AND LET IT BE"
TUNE: HENDON

We have come to hear anew
　　Your "old story," tried and true.
And my words of truth and grace
　　Are alive and always new,
　　When you grow in faithfulness.

We have come to know anew
　　Your redemptive news for us.
And my words of love and strength
　　Are alive and always new,
　　When you grow in pray'rfulness.

We have come to learn anew
　　Your salvation's precious cost.
And my words of joy and pow'r
　　Are alive and always new,
　　When you grow in humbleness.

We have come to love anew
　　Christ our Lord who died for us.
And his words of light and life
　　Are alive and always new,
　　When you grow in gratitude.

Save Us, We Beseech Thee

Psalm 118:19–29;   *Luke 19:28–40*

Open to us the gates of righteousness that we may enter and give you thanks.
> You are our God, and we will bless you.
>> Hosanna! Hosanna!

This is the "gate of the Lord," my gate,
> **and the righteous shall enter through it.**
>> **Bind the festal procession with branches.**

We thank you that you have answered us and have become our salvation.
> Save us, we beseech thee, O Lord!
>> Hosanna! Hosanna!

The stone which the builders rejected has become the chief cornerstone.
> **If you were silent, the very stones would cry out:**
>> **"Hosanna! Hosanna!"**

Blessed be the one who enters in the name of the Lord!
> You are our God and have given us light.
>> You are good and your love endures forever.

Let the children sing their songs of joy!
> **Today there is peace in heaven and glory in the highest.**
>> **What a marvelous sight!**

As Christ neared the city, all the disciples and multitude rejoiced
> and praised you with a loud voice.
>> The teachers there said, "Rebuke your disciples."

And Christ said, "I tell you, if these were silent, the very stones would cry out."
> **This is my day; rejoice and be glad in it.**
>> **My goodness and my love endure forever.**

Words by Anne McKinstry. From *Breathing New Life into Lent, Volume 3,* copyright 2000 by Judson Press. Used by permission.

The City Gates Are Open Wide

Psalms 118:19–29;   Luke 19:28–40

HYMN: "'TIS MIDNIGHT AND ON OLIVE'S BROW"
TUNE: OLIVE'S BROW

The city gates are open wide;
    Hosannas sweetly fill the air.
If silenced, then the stones would cry:
    The Man of Sorrows enters now.

The city gates are open wide;
    And palms, so flowing, fill the way.
The children, so delighted, sing:
    The man who loves us passes by.

The city gates are open wide;
    And garments deck the royal road.
This is the day that I have made;
    Rejoice, this is a marv'lous sight.

The city gates are open wide;
    Hosannas sweetly fill the air.
If silenced, then the stones would cry:
    The Man of Sorrows enters now.

Gather Around My Table

1 Corinthians 11:23–26;   *John 13:1–17*

It means so much to us to hear you say,
    "This is my body, broken for you." How we hunger for this.
Gather around my table and take this bread,
    remembering my costly love. All things are ready.

The world can be so cold and lonely.
    How we long to have John's warm place upon your breast.
Lay your heads upon my warm and generous bosom.
    There is room for all desiring closeness.

It means so much to us to hear you say,
    "This cup is the new covenant in my blood." We are thirsty.
Gather around my table and drink this cup,
    always remembering my love and sacrifice.

We desire to be "clean all over," and like Peter we say,
    "Wash our hands and heads, as well as our feet."
My basin and towel are a symbol of pureness as well as service.
    Become clean as new snow in this washing.

There is a deep lostness and hunger within us.
    We are overjoyed to be invited to gather around your table.
Eat and drink this holy meal with a deep gratitude
    for all that God has done for you.

Words by Anne McKinstry. From *Breathing New Life into Lent, Volume 3,* copyright 2000 by Judson Press. Used by permission.

Maundy Thursday

We Are Weak and Hungry

1 Corinthians 11:23–26;   John 13:1–17

HYMN: "NOW THE DAY IS OVER"
TUNE: MERRIAL

We are weak and hungry,
    Children needing food.
Gather 'round my table;
    All things are prepared.

We are cold and lonely,
    Children needing warmth.
Lay your heads upon me;
    There is room for all.

We are sad and sinful,
    Children needing you.
Eat this bread of mercy;
    Drink this cup of life.

We are soiled and weary,
    Children needing truth.
Nearby is my basin;
    You'll feel pure as snow.

We are lost and hungry,
    Children needing love.
Gather 'round my table;
    All things are prepared.

Be Glad in That Which I Create

Isaiah 65:17–25;   1 Corinthians 15:19–26

We want to become a "new Jerusalem,"
    a people who are glad and full of rejoicing.
Each dawn I am creating a new heaven and a new earth.
    Be glad in that which I create.

We want to become a "new Jerusalem,"
    a people who are penitent and who are forgiven.
Each dawn I am creating a place of rejoicing.
    Former sins shall not be remembered.

We want to become a "new Jerusalem,"
    a people from whom there is no cry of distress.
Each dawn I am creating a tearless morning.
    There shall be no sound of weeping.

We want to become a "new Jerusalem,"
    the offspring of the blessed of the Lord.
Each dawn I am creating a Jerusalem at peace;
    and you shall not destroy on this holy hill.

We want to become a "new Jerusalem,"
    a people alive in Christ with resurrection power.
Each dawn I am creating a new heaven and earth
    where death has no power. Your Savior lives!

Each Dawn Your Light Arrives

Isaiah 65:17–25;   1 Corinthians 15:19–26

HYMN: "WHEN MORNING GILDS THE SKIES"
TUNE: LAUDES DOMNI

Each dawn your light arrives,
Awak'ning us who sleep, with resurrection pow'r.
My heav'n and earth are new.
Rejoice, Jerusalem! Your Savior lives again.

Each dawn your truth arrives,
Refreshing us who doubt, with resurrection pow'r.
Your former sins are gone.
Rejoice, Jerusalem! Your Savior lives again.

Each dawn your love arrives,
Embracing us who weep, with resurrection pow'r.
No more shall there be tears.
Rejoice, Jerusalem! Your Savior lives again.

Each dawn your peace arrives,
Releasing us who boast, with resurrection pow'r.
No more shall there be war.
Rejoice, Jerusalem! Your Savior lives again.

Each dawn your Christ arrives,
Reviving us who die, with resurrection pow'r.
No more shall there be death.
Rejoice, Jerusalem! Your Savior lives again.

Section III

NEW SONGS FOR LENT

by Janet E. Powers

Introduction

This section offers original, never-before-published songs for Lenten praise and worship. They are provided especially for churches that like to include contemporary music in their worship services. The music and lyrics for the songs are the creative work of Rev. Janet E. Powers.

In general, the songs are simple and easy to learn. They can be performed by individuals or small groups as preservice music or during the service itself. A church might choose one song to teach the congregation at each service in order to provide a sense of thematic unity.

For the Season of Lent

We Are Like Clay

Janet E. Powers

We are like clay shaped in-to ves-sels;— We are like clay where trea-sure's stored. And it is God Who forms and

This song is a good reminder of *whose* we are. The season of Lent reminds us that we are in perpetual need of reshaping by the Master Potter.

First Sunday in Lent

To You, I'll Sing My Praise

Janet E. Powers

A song of praise, to be used near the beginning of worship or as a commitment-response to the sermon or the offering.

Gather Us, Lord

Janet E. Powers

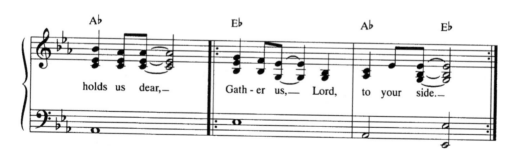

Use this song as a call to worship or as opening praise music.

Zechariah's Song

Janet E. Powers

The lectionary passages bring to mind Zechariah's blessing at Jesus' birth. Jesus is a Light, indeed, even in the shadow-season of Lent.

Third Week in Lent

Come to Me

Janet E. Powers

These lyrics are taken from Isaiah 55, to be used as preparation for the reading of Scripture or as an invitation to the Lord's Table.

Fourth Week in Lent

Shepherd of Love

Janet E. Powers

Manna from heaven, forgiveness freely offered, one who eats with sinners–is this not a Shepherd of love? Use this song as opening praise music or as an assurance of pardon.

For the Sky

Janet E. Powers

May the Spir - it___ show - er___ us___ with
Love,___ with Love,___ with Love.___ Let it
be,___ let it be,___ let it___ be.___

This is a song of praise with images as rich and diverse as the lectionary readings of this week. Sing gently but not too slowly.

Teach Us, Lord

Janet E. Powers

Sing this song before the reading of Scripture or prior to the sermon.

Weep No More

Janet E. Powers

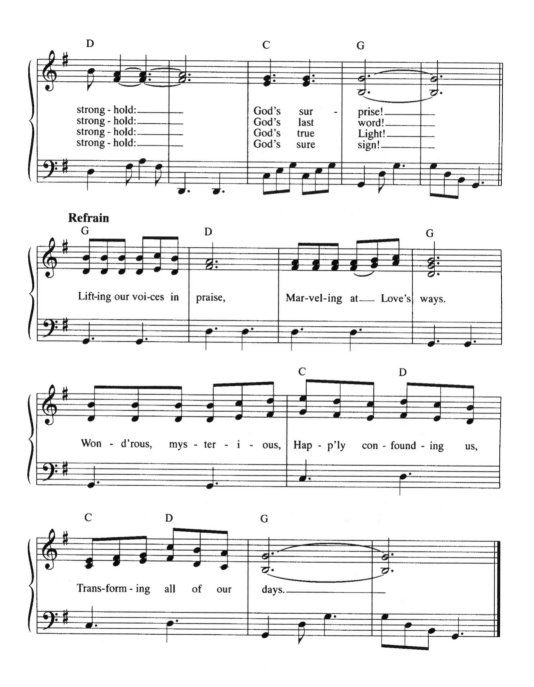

strong - hold:____ God's sur - prise!____
strong - hold:____ God's last word!____
strong - hold:____ God's true Light!____
strong - hold:____ God's sure sign!____

Refrain

Lift-ing our voi-ces in praise, Mar-vel-ing at__ Love's ways.

Won - d'rous, mys - ter - i - ous, Hap - p'ly con - found - ing us,

Trans-form - ing all of our days.____

Sing this chorus in response to the Gospel reading or near the close of worship.

Amos 6:24

Janet E. Powers

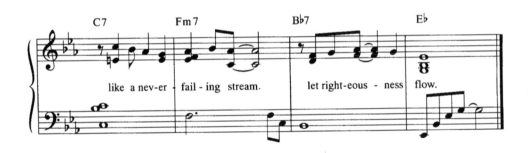

Jesus' resurrection has implications for the immediate present, not just the distant future. "Let justice pour down!" is a response to God's justice in the resurrection.